T0290092

Language and Truth

Language and Truth

A study of the Sanskrit language and its relationship with principles of truth

PAUL DOUGLAS

SHEPHEARD-WALWYN (PUBLISHERS) LTD

© 2010 Paul Douglas

All rights reserved. No part of this book may be reproduced in any form without the written permission of the publisher, Shepheard-Walwyn (Publishers) Ltd

First published in 2010 by
Shepheard-Walwyn (Publishers) Ltd
107 Parkway House, Sheen Lane
London SW14 8LS

British Library Cataloguing in Publication Data
A catalogue record of this book
is available from the British Library

ISBN-13: 978-0-85683-271-0

Typeset by Arthouse Publishing Solutions Ltd,
Alderton, Suffolk
Printed and bound through
s|s| media limited, Wallington, Surrey

Contents

Pronunciation guide vi
Introduction vii

1. Different premises on which language may be founded 1
2. How may different languages relate to truth? 10
3. Basic elements of language as evident in Sanskrit 27
4. Words: their formation and classes 41
5. Sentences and relationships within them 57
6. Sound, word and meaning. What is meaning? 69
7. Pāṇinian grammar: some special features 85
8. Laws of Sanskrit reflecting natural laws? 100

Appendix 1. The credentials of Sanskrit 108
Appendix 2. The extent of Sandhi 109
Bibliography 114
Index 115

Pronunciation Guide

Almost all Sanskrit words appear in italics in the text and may then be sounded in accordance with this pronunciation guide.

a	final a in 'Rāma'	ṅ	n in 'bungalow'
ā	a in 'dart'	c	ch in 'church'
i	i in 'it'	ch	chh in 'beachhead'
ī	ee in 'peel'	ñ	n in same mouth position as ch
u	u in 'pull'	ṭ ṭh ḍ ḍh ṇ	tip of tongue in roof of mouth
ū	oo in 'pool'	v	w
ṛ	ri in 'Krishna'	ś	sh
ḷ	lry in 'revelry'	ṣ	sh with tip of tongue in roof of mouth
e	a in 'late'		
ai	y in 'my'	ṁ	nasal only through nose before a sibilant
o	o in 'open'		
au	ow in 'vow'	ḥ	breath at end (*visarga*) e.g. ah

The aspirated consonants eg kh, jh, th, dh are sounded with breath through the k, j etc.

All other letters are written and sounded as in English.

Emphasis should be placed on long vowels and on short vowels which are followed by conjunct consonants. For example the first 'a' of *pratyaya* is emphasised because it is followed by two consonants.

Introduction

THE aim in this book is to explore what relationship there may be between language and truth. That deceptively simple word, 'truth', can be understood in various ways, but for the purpose of this book, it is taken as understood in the philosophy of Advaita (Non-dualism). More particularly, a good part of the book discusses ways in which one language, Sanskrit, can be seen as embodying the principles of Advaita.

I took up the study of Sanskrit some thirty years ago, having been led to this by the Advaitic teaching of Śrī Śāntānanda Sarasvatī, Shankaracharya of Jyotir Math from 1961 – 85. This teaching was given in conversations* with Leon MacLaren, founder and former leader of the School of Economic Science in London. In particular I was struck by one statement: 'The grammatical rules of Sanskrit are also the rules of the creation.' This has been an enduring interest while studying the language, but it took some time to realise the obvious fact that the statement can only really begin to be critically examined and understood when there is a thorough knowledge of Sanskrit grammar. That has necessitated penetration of the master Sanskrit grammarian, Pāṇini, whose classic work, the *Aṣṭādhyāyī*, with nearly 4000 sutras or succinct statements of law, was composed in the 5th century BCE. That study has proceeded slowly but steadily in the company of fellow students in the School, and much has been appreciated along the way. It may therefore be worthwhile setting down what has been discovered to provide a staging post on the way to a full understanding of the statement and its practical application.

* These conversations are unpublished and the rights are reserved.

We have been guided in these studies by the words of Śrī Śāntānanda Sarasvatī, who has made a number of mind-provoking statements about the Sanskrit language. For example:

> 'Sanskrit has all its words full of spiritual significance.'

> 'The truth was originally declared through the Sanskrit language, and it still holds the truth in its original form.'

> 'Sanskrit is refined and truly natural for it contains original laws and original sounds and their combinations.'

I would like to thank Annick Hardaker, Helen Harper, Brian Hodgkinson, and Reverend Dr Stephen Thompson for providing me with very helpful comments on drafts of the book, and for their encouragement. I must also thank S M Jaiswal for the inspiring lead he has given over the years in investigating the philosophy of the Sanskrit language, and acknowledge that the vision and teaching of Leon MacLaren in my initial years of Sanskrit study have provided a firm foundation and direction for all later studies.

Chapter 1

Different premises on which language may be founded

1.1 Various views and explanations of language have been expressed over the ages. Each depends on the premise on which it is founded. It is not the purpose of this book to investigate these premises, but it may help set the scene to give a brief description of how language is seen from certain premises, including particularly the Advaitic premise.

Advaita

Advaita is a Sanskrit word which translates as Non-duality. The Advaitic premise is that reality or truth is one, totally still, yet all-pervasive, pure, omniscient, partless, conscious and self-existent. The apparent multiplicity of the world is not real. In truth it is one. The seen is no different from the seer, as in a dream. The multiplicity is in name and form only. These forms reflect the unity to a greater or lesser extent, as in humans, animals, plants and stones. Our true nature is identical with the nature of the One Self. The nature of the One, the Self, the Absolute, God, Brahman, is existence, consciousness and bliss – *sat, cit, ānanda* in Sanskrit. The universe appears as an expression of the nature of the Absolute, through the powers or forces of the Absolute. This manifestation has three stages or worlds: causal or spiritual; subtle or mental/emotional; and physical/material. When any of these terms are used in this book, they refer to the relevant world.

1.2 An Advaitic View of Language

How then can there be an Advaitic view of language? In the same way as there is an Advaitic view of the world. This oneness is expressed by sound in the natural language. The sounds we can hear in human language are not that natural language, but are reflections of it, however distorted.

The world is an expression of the substance of the One as name and form. This creative process begins with Om (ॐ), the original causal Word, sound or vibration of energy. The opening statement of the *Māṇḍūkya* Upanishad says: 'The Word ॐ is the Imperishable; all this its manifestation. Past, present, future – everything is ॐ. Whatever transcends the three divisions of time, that too is ॐ.' Originally there is only one word or vibration, yet this word continues to sound throughout the universe. There are obvious parallels with the opening statement of the Gospel of St John, 'In the beginning was the Word, and the Word was with God, and the Word was God', and at the material level with the view of astrophysicists that the universe began with an enormous explosion of energy which is still vibrating and expanding. Bhartṛhari, a language philosopher who lived in India in the 5th century CE., described the first step in language as a flash of consciousness called a *sphoṭa*, literally, 'an explosion in consciousness'.

The universe is said to be spoken into existence. 'God indeed was one and alone. Speech was his own being. Speech was the second to him. He said, "Let me send forth this speech. She will go and become all these various things." ' (*Kathaka Saṁhitā*) 'All transformation has speech as its basis, and it is name only.' (*Chāndogya* Upanishad 6.1.4) A twentieth century exposition of this was given by Śāntānanda Sarasvatī: 'Brahman is the word and the word is Brahman. The consciousness first originates as word. The subtlest form becomes coarse. The word is subtle and things are coarse.... World comes out of the word and, having existed, it will merge into the word as systematically as it appeared from the word' (1991 Day 5). This is why creation is said to be formed with and maintained by the natural language, the grammar of which is the natural law, *dharma*.

The sound or vibration of energy which gives rise to everything in this universe arises in consciousness and is eternal. The sounds arising through air as in human speech, are in space and are transient. Human language is a reflection of the natural language, even though it may be a distorted one. In human language words, said to be eternal in essence by Bhartṛhari and other Advaitists, find expression in stages, from the subtlest level to the final stage of speech. In this system the sentence is an expression of the unity, one indivisible whole, while the analysis of the parts of a sentence and of individual words is just to help with understanding. Close attention to pronunciation and grammar is necessary for appreciation of subtler levels of meaning and spiritual significance. With this close attention the all-pervading consciousness becomes more apparent.

In this view, the form and sound of a language determines how far it can express and reflect the truth. Language lawfully formed has the capacity to reflect the natural laws of the universe. Sound is held to be of fundamental importance, and the qualities of sounds in the basic elements of a language, such as its alphabet, therefore go a long way to determining the real differences between languages, and their capacity to reflect the truth.

1.3 Views of Language in the West

In the West, the Middle East and the Far East greater emphasis has been given to the written word, in contrast to the Indian subcontinent. Indeed the word 'grammar' originally meant 'the art of writing'. Much attention has been paid to the calligraphic arts in Christian, Islamic and Chinese civilisations, even after printing was originally invented in the 12th to 13th centuries in China and greatly developed in the 15th century in the West. On the other hand, the science of phonetics was much more highly developed in the Indian sub-continent in the millennium before Christ. Four of the six branches of the Veda, called Vedāngas, are concerned with language, the first being pronunciation or phonetics, the second chanting or metrics, the third grammar, and the fourth etymology.

Among the earliest known views on language expressed in the West are those to be found in the writings of Plato and Aristotle in the 4th century BCE. Very broadly the Platonic view could be classified as rationalist and the Aristotelian view as empirical. In the Platonic dialogues, the theory is developed that visible objects are passing representations of long-lasting or ever-lasting ideas. A particular car lasts for a certain time and then is destroyed or disintegrates, whereas the word 'car' continues, and while it continues further physical cars can be created. If truth is equated with eternity then the word 'car' is closer to truth than a physical car, and in a way is the cause of the physical car. Aristotle took the view that the relationship between words and objects consisted of resemblance and convention. Words represent objects, and there is a convention about which words represent which objects. Augustine in the 4th Century CE, reiterated the view that words represent, and signify, objects.

Mediaeval philosophers were interested in what thought and language are, and how they arise. There were two main theories about thought. The Aristotelian view, held by the earlier philosophers such as Aquinas in the 13th century, was that the mind takes on the same form as the things represented, and presents likenesses or pictures of them. A table in a room and in the mind are the same thing under two different forms of existence. Words describe this thing. Later mediaeval philosophers, such as Ockham in the 14th century, held that intuitive cognitions produce concepts which have objective existence in the mind and are caused by the objects they represent. Again words are descriptive. In both views the world holds a multiplicity of objects, whether physical or mental, and there are a multiplicity of minds experiencing them.

1.4 An Empirical View of Language

With a decline in the authority of the Church, modern Western philosophy began in the sixteenth and seventeenth centuries with philosophers such as Descartes and Spinoza, who used reason as their guide, and were therefore called rationalists. However by the end of the seventeenth century this view, which produced a number of conflicting philosophical explanations, was being discredited. The view which emerged in striking contrast both to the rationalist and Advaitic views, and which has continued to the present day, is the empirical view. This is based on the premise that the world and its multiplicity are real, with all knowledge coming initially from sensory experiences of the world. Language is derived from this source and is not innate. For example John Locke, the 17th century English philosopher, believed that simple ideas come directly from sensory experience, and complex or abstract ideas, such as 'man' or 'beauty' are based on a number of simple ideas. Complex ideas are made by abstracting common characteristics from special characteristics of individual things, for example, experiences of different men from which one deduces the idea of 'man'. These ideas all derive ultimately from sensations either from within or from outside the mind. To the empiricist words are articulated sounds used as signs or labels for ideas. There is no natural connection between the sounds and the ideas.

In the 19th and 20th centuries, with the increasing scientific emphasis on empirical forms of investigation, the empirical view of language grew in strength. In the first half of the 20th century philosophical schools of thought such as logical positivism (sometimes called logical empiricism) concentrated on the investigation of language. Such philosophers were concerned with identifying the truth or otherwise of statements, but as their premise was that a proposition only has a meaning if there is in principle a means of verifying it, they rejected all theological, metaphysical and ethical statements as lacking in meaning. One famous conclusion of A.J. Ayer was that no proposition can be more than a probable hypothesis. It is a little ironic that his most famous book was entitled Language, Truth and Logic, very similar to the title of this book, but with a very different perspective.

Some modern linguists have extended the empirical premise to grammar, and regard the structure and form of language as deriving from common usage. How language is used and developed in ordinary speech is the determining factor for what is correct usage. Grammatical rules are only significant if they are in common use. If they are not normally used, they are not relevant. In this way dialects are given full acknowledgement, and grammar reflects common usage, rather than the other way round. Laws of grammar in this sense are more customs than laws, and liable to frequent change.

1.5 A Rationalist View of Language

In the last half century there has been a radical turn away from such views of language in some quarters. One significant trend has been a reconnection with the rationalist approach of Descartes and Kant for example and, even further back, of Plato. The premise here is that the essence of language is innate in all humans. Its source is within, not without.

The most famous exponent of this view, currently, is Noam Chomsky, who has introduced concepts such as 'universal grammar' and 'generative grammar'. For him the human mind has the inherent knowledge of, or 'competence' in, a universal grammar common to all humans. It is the genetic component of the language faculty of humans. The individual then learns to use and express this in a particular language or languages through particular grammars. Language is seen as a 'mirror of the mind' in the sense that it mirrors and expresses the innate properties of human intelligence. All human languages must conform in some way with the universal grammar, as this grammar is directly related to how the mind works. It is interesting to note that this bears some similarity to Bhartṛhari's philosophy of language in the 5th century. Iyer, in his study of Bhartṛhari, says: 'The central idea of his philosophy, that the ultimate Reality is of the nature of the word, which presupposes consciousness, has resulted in the notion that all of us are born with the source of valid knowledge and of speech within us.' [1]

One of Chomsky's descriptions of universal grammar is 'the conditions that must be met by the grammars of all human languages, and this includes universal phonetics (sound) and universal semantics (meaning).'[2] Universal and particular grammars are linked by generative grammar, where concepts such as 'deep structure' and 'surface structure' are used. For example, the two sentences, 'He is eager to please', and 'He is easy to please', have the same surface structure, but a different deep structure. Who is doing the pleasing?

Recent developments in genetics have given support to this view that language structure is innate in humans, with the identification of a human gene which shapes the larynx in such a way that breath passing through it can be controlled by the mind to form speech. Individuals with damage to this gene are unable to speak properly. The gene is believed to have arisen through mutation about the same time as humans became a distinct species. When humans subsequently began to develop specialised social and creative activities, these have been seen as indications of the development of speech.

1.6 Another modern view of language

Even such a brief glimpse of some different views of language as this would not be complete without some mention of the most significant language philosopher of the last century, Ludwig Wittgenstein. In his first book, the Tractatus, he maintained the view that words, or rather sentences, were pictures of the real world, the structure of the world determined the structure of sentences. This led him to conclude that only statements of fact were meaningful, and ethical, artistic and philosophical statements had no real meaning. In his later works he put forward a contrary view, that the structure of our sentences determines our view of the world. Here language is analogous to a tool, not a picture. From this perspective he argued that language is one among many forms of human activity and that words and sentences are deeds, their meaning being their 'use', 'function', 'aim' and 'role'. Their use is settled by publicly agreed rules, there being no such thing as a private language. For example, the sentence 'This is a king', referring to a chess piece, will only convey more meaning than a particularly shaped object if the hearer knows what a board game is, knows the concept of a chess piece and has learnt to play chess just from observation or also knows the rules of the game. He spoke of 'language games' and of language as 'part of a form of life', 'an outward social phenomenon'. He spent much time examining individual words such as 'mean', 'know', 'beautiful', 'expect', 'pain' and 'toothache', in a way which supported this view. This bears some similarity to discussions in the Platonic Dialogues about 'justice', 'courage', 'temperance' etc. although his discussions, unlike Plato's, led to meanings dependent on use , not meanings dependent on an idea and supported by reason.

1.7 Where next?

Each of these views of language leads to a different way of approaching the question of how language is related to truth. We will follow the Advaitic approach, and start with an initial comparison of how different languages measure up to that approach.

Notes

1 *Bhartṛhari* K A S Iyer Deccan College 1992
2 *Language and Mind,* Third Edition, Noam Chomsky Cambridge University Press 2006

Chapter 2

How may different languages relate to truth?

2.1 Languages may be classified, and therefore compared, in various ways. Some of these classifications will be mentioned here, but none of them enables us to address directly the relation of languages to truth. What criteria should be used? Capacity to meet communication needs, sophistication of grammatical structure, beauty of sound, fineness of literature? Attempts by the academic community to evaluate languages as 'higher' or 'lower' have never led to any lasting agreement, and nowadays these attempts have been largely abandoned. For example, some languages of 'primitive' cultures are now recognised to have a grammatical complexity as great as those of 'civilised' cultures, and are equally able to meet the communication needs of their society.

Nevertheless, several languages are certainly regarded as special by those who use them, for reasons of philosophy and religion, including Sanskrit, Arabic and classical Hebrew. As an example, here is a translation of an extract from The Corpus Hermeticum, an Egyptian text, believed to have been composed between the 1st and 3rd centuries CE:

> 'When expressed in its original language, the text preserves the pure spirit of the words. For the very quality of the sound and the pronunciation of this Egyptian language carries in itself the power of what is spoken.' (Asclepius to King Ammon)[1]

Asclepius goes on to warn against translation into Greek because of its 'arrogant, loose and showy style.' The supporters of a particular language may see its special nature lying in a combination of a refined grammar, beauty, and deep significance of its sounds, and its ability to express the truth as they understand it. Yet, while one language may be cited as having special and valuable characteristics of this nature, this does not mean that other languages are bereft of such characteristics.

2.2 Different types of language

Linguists have identified different types of language by considering their characteristics such as grammatical structure, word forms, and their sounds. Most languages are a mixture of these types, with a tendency towards one type. Three of the commonest are:

Inflectional. A number of classical languages are called inflectional or synthetic languages. Their principle characteristic is the substantial use of affixes and case endings to indicate meaning and role in the sentence. The internal form of words carries most of the meaning. Word order and pitch are less important than in other types of language. Examples of such languages are Latin, Greek, Arabic and Sanskrit.

Analytical. On the other hand, there are analytical or isolating languages. These have no word endings or affixes. Relationships within a meaningful unit of communication, i.e. a sentence, are shown by word order, particles, pitch and tone. A good example of such a language is Mandarin Chinese. A line of Mandarin appears simply as a number of distinct symbols.

Agglutinative. In agglutinative languages, words are made up of parts stuck or glued together, each of which has a particular grammatical meaning. This can be seen clearly in Turkish, Finnish, Swahili and, to a lesser extent, Japanese. For example, the Swahili word *anayenipatia (maji)* means 'he who gets (water) for me.' This is composed of *a* (he), *na* (present tense), *ye* (who), *ni* (me), *pat* (get), *ia* (for).

Classifying by type is a rather blunt way of distinguishing languages, as they usually contain elements of several types. It can be more informative to say what principles are more important in a language, such as word form (morphology) or word order (syntax). Sanskrit clearly places more importance on word form and English on word order. Hardly any change in word order is possible in the following English sentence without losing its meaning: 'The man will eat the fruit', but in the equivalent Sanskrit sentence, *naraḥ phalam khādiṣyati*, the words can be in any order, as the full meaning is carried in the form of the words.

Languages can be classified in other ways.

Phonological. Languages which emphasise particular types of sounds, such as open sounds (vowels), stops (consonants), syllables (stops with open sounds), clicks, pitch, stress, nasal sounds.

Historical. Languages with a common ancestor, such as the Indo-European languages – most modern European languages, Hindi, Urdu, Gujurati, Latin, Greek, Sanskrit, Farsi; Sino-Tibetan languages e.g. Mandarin; Semitic e.g Arabic and Hebrew; Dravidian e.g. Tamil.

Geographical. The geographical extent over which a language is or was used. English is currently by far the most widely used language across the world. Two thousand years ago that language would have been classical Latin in the Western world. In the East it might have been Sanskrit, which spread across South-East Asia into China and Japan carrying Hinduism, Jainism, and particularly Buddhism.

Statistical. The number of people speaking a language. At present the language most spoken as a first language is Mandarin, although when second language is taken into account, it is English.

However, apart from the first of these classifications, none is relevant to the identification of any relationship with truth. That brings us back to the question at the beginning of the chapter – how to relate languages to truth. As this book concentrates on the Advaitic understanding of truth, let us start to explore that relationship.

2.3 Relationship of three languages to truth.

Having identified how the phrase 'different languages' in the chapter heading can be interpreted, I will interpret the second part of the heading, 'truth', in accordance with Advaita philosophy as described in chapter 1.1 and 1.2. This clears the ground for a broad comparison of three very different languages, Sanskrit, English and Mandarin. Sanskrit has been chosen because it appears to be the most fruitful language to which this question can be addressed. The exploration of this language will also continue in subsequent chapters. English and Mandarin have been chosen partly because they are the two most spoken languages in the world today, and partly because they differ significantly from Sanskrit and each other in their construction.

Sanskrit, an Indo-European language, is largely an inflectional language. Word form is far more important than word order. Word formation involves a substantial grammar, which charts the development of words step by step from their initial root, called a *dhātu*, through the addition of suffixes, called *pratyaya*s, to their fully inflected form. Even when words are fully inflected, their initial and final syllables continue to change due to laws of sound combination called *sandhi*. The language is also highly organised phonologically, with a consistency and precisely ordered structure in the sounds it uses. New words are based on Sanskrit *dhātu*s and *pratyaya*s, and are not simply an incorporation of a foreign word in its original form.

English, like Sanskrit, is an Indo-European language, and therefore has some affinity with Sanskrit. Originally it was a highly inflected language, but over the last thousand years it has lost much of this, and is now mainly an analytical language, where word order is more important than word form. During this time it has been significantly influenced by other languages, particularly Norman French and Latin, and, during the time of the British Empire, by words from languages used in the Empire. Such words have usually been incorporated in their original, or slightly modified, Anglicised form. The effect has been a great expansion in vocabulary, and a divergence between the spoken and written forms. This divergence also derives from changes in the pronunciation of vowels which took place about five hundred years ago.

Mandarin, a Sino-Tibetan language, is very different from both English and Sanskrit. It is very analytical, and word order is therefore very important. It does not have an alphabet. Instead, it uses many thousands of characters. Each character is a syllable or sometimes a whole word, a pictogram or ideogram. There are no inflections, and affixes are separate characters. Consequently, nouns and verbs have only one form, leaving number, tense, case and gender to be indicated by particles. Most words consist of two characters. One is the root, and the second conveys the phonetic element, the tone. There are four tones and these distinguish words which use the same radical character. For example the root 'ma' can mean 'mother', 'hemp', 'horse', or 'scold' depending on the tone used. The character for 'ma' is the same, but each tone carrying the sound is indicated by a different character. There is little relationship between a root character and a sound, as there is no alphabet.

To identify how far a language has characteristics in tune with Advaitic principles of truth, we need to refer to the summary of those principles set out in chapter 1. The ones that seem particularly relevant to language are, in no particular order of significance, unity, sound, lawfulness, consciousness, reflectivity and stability. The meaning being given to each of these very broad concepts is explained as we proceed.

2.4 Unity

The unity of a language is shown by it having a stable base, lawful development of words, providing cohesion, harmonious sounds and an expression which shows unity in diversity. As stability, lawfulness and sound are dealt with later as distinct principles, I will concentrate here on how unity may be seen in the diversity of the language.

In Sanskrit, as words are formed from *dhātu*s (roots) and *pratyaya*s (suffixes), with each step laid down by grammatical laws, they can be seen to develop from simple to highly complex forms, with a far greater complexity of laws applying as the word nears its final form. At various points the principle of expressing diversity within unity is evident. For example, each *dhātu* generates many words through the addition of *pratyaya*s and prefixes. The *dhātu kṛ* (nearest English pronunciation 'kri') 'to do or make' generates many hundreds of verbal and nominal forms. In the classic Monier-Williams Sanskrit dictionary there are seventeen columns of words derived from this *dhātu*. At the heart of all of them is this one sound *kṛ*. Another example of unity may be seen in the pervasiveness of the sound *a*, the first and principal letter of the Sanskrit alphabet. It is by far the most common letter in *dhātu*s and *pratyaya*s; it is used in prefixes to express the negative and the past tense; and it appears in over half of noun case affixes and in over two thirds of verbal affixes.

In writing, symbols have to be added to consonants to indicate either no vowel at all or the addition of any vowel except *a*. The third example of unity is the pervasiveness of *sandhi* which modifies the sound of words so that they come together to form a harmonious whole in sentences. For example *īśā upaniṣad* becomes *īśopaniśad*. This principle operates throughout Sanskrit, so that words are shaped by it, and sentences change their form substantially in accordance with rules of *sandhi*.

As English is largely an analytical language, and Mandarin even more so, they both use many more words to communicate. These words change their form little, but depend on order and, in Mandarin, tone, for understanding. For example, in the last two sentences only six out of 36 words have changed their form, to indicate number: 'is' 'they' 'words' (2) 'these' and 'their'. With much less emphasis on how words are formed, the sense of expression from simple to highly complex forms, and from unity to diversity, is much less evident. In English there is hardly any explicit recognition of the principles of *sandhi* operating to bind words together in a sentence – only the one example of 'an' in this paragraph. In Mandarin the concept of tonal *sandhi* is recognised within words, so that, for example, a dipping tone changes to a rising tone before another dipping tone.

2.5 Sound

Sound is of course fundamental to language, but it is also fundamental to a universe which starts with vibration and expands through vibration. What sound vibrations make up any language are therefore of great importance. The basic sound elements of languages such as Sanskrit and English are the letters of the alphabet, out of which all words are formed. In Mandarin there is no alphabet, but many thousands of characters, which are sounded variously and in different tones.

In Sanskrit great importance is placed on sound, including proper pronunciation. The sounds and order of the alphabet have special characteristics. Letters of the alphabet are grouped into families according to the exact position in the vocal apparatus where they are sounded, and the particular method of articulation. For example, the first vowel, *a*, is sounded in the throat, and is a guttural sound. Being sounded in the throat, *a* could not be sounded like 'a' in 'game' which uses both guttural and palatal positions. Time measures are also distinguished for vowels, so long *ā*, twice the length of short *a*, would sound like the 'a' in 'part'. One of the consequences of this is that each letter is sounded in a consistent way. The written form of the language reflects the oral form exactly.

Although the English alphabet uses many sounds also used in Sanskrit, the alphabet gives little sense of order, and individual letters may be pronounced in a variety of ways, depending on custom and practice, history and geography. For example, in the last sentence 'a' is pronounced in five different ways and 'e' in six, when the standard English dialect is used. The ways in which English is pronounced around the world vary greatly, and even within quite small geographical areas, dialects can make a big difference. This may partly stem from the absence of a strong tradition of correct pronunciation for much of its life.

As Mandarin does not have an alphabet to maintain some consistency in sound, it is not surprising that the same written characters are sounded quite differently in different geographical areas, leading to non-comprehension in speech between regions. The multiplicity of characters is another factor encouraging changes in sounds over time. On the other hand, in the 7th and 8th centuries, with the spread of Sanskrit into China through Buddhism, Mandarin scholars devoted their attention to exploring the sounds of Mandarin with a view to analysing and systematising them. Also, the great importance placed on tones to convey meaning has left its effect in the noticeable ability of Mandarin speakers to sound in perfect pitch.

2.6 Lawfulness

Everything in the universe is subject to law, and this applies to human behaviour and an individual's mental and emotional states, as well as the natural world. It must therefore be fundamental to language. Every language has grammatical laws, but the extent to which these are comprehensive, stable, recognised, and followed, and express coherent principles varies greatly. Languages which are shaped largely by changing common usage could be said to be governed by a less conscious and more opaque level of law than those with a coherent and ordered grammar.

Every step in the development of a Sanskrit word is lawful, and described in the grammar. The fact that these steps are described and taught in Sanskrit grammatical works means that they are acknowledged and maintained. It also means that each word can be analysed to understand how the combination of its component parts contributes to its meaning. For example, the word translated as 'truth' is *satyam*. This word consists of the present participle *sat* 'being' from the *dhātu as* 'to be', plus the *pratyaya yam*, which has the sense of 'excellent for'. So the word for truth in Sanskrit literally means 'excellent for being', an interesting understanding of the concept of truth.

English certainly has a comprehensive grammar, which is largely coherent (except perhaps in spelling, for historical reasons), but it has changed over the centuries. At times grammar has been held in low repute, and allowed to follow common usage rather than the other way round. Although English is an Indo-European language and has much in common with

Sanskrit, including some of its grammar, there are a number of elements in Sanskrit grammar related to Advaita which are not explicitly recognised in English grammar, as subsequent chapters will show.

Mandarin, being a highly analytical language, with few inflective or agglutinative features, has a grammar which resides more in word order and tone than in the forms of the words themselves. This leaves little scope for law in the formation of words or in combinations of words into compound words. For example, future and past are expressed by distinct particles. The isolationist nature of the language, as expressed in its thousands of distinct characters, does not encourage words to accommodate to each other in sound, at least in any formal and recognised way, except in tone.

2.7 Consciousness

Human language is possibly the most powerful tool created by man. Without language there would be no civilisation or culture, and scientific investigation would be minimal. Most of the features of human society, being based on moral laws and customs and on reasoned scientific investigation, would not exist. There is a case for saying that speech is what distinguishes mankind from animals, as the development of speech took place in parallel with the emergence of social and creative activities. For language to develop, a certain level of consciousness is necessary. Although consciousness cannot be seen, its effects certainly can, and these can be compared as more or less conscious. This comparison may be applied to languages, and what has been expressed in them.

The three languages currently being discussed all have many fine works, which are evidence of a high level of consciousness. In English, for example, there are the Authorised Version of the Bible; Shakespeare's works; the poetry of Chaucer, Milton, Wordsworth, T. S Eliot, and many others; the philosophy of Locke, Hume, Emerson, James and Dewey; and the speeches of Lincoln, Churchill and Kennedy. In Sanskrit there have been many philosophical and religious works, such as the Upanishads, the Bhagavad Gītā, the Brahma Sutras, and the works of Shankara; and the great epics such as the Mahābhārata and the Rāmāyaṇa. Mandarin also has its great philosophers such as Confucius, Lao-Tse, Mencius, Zhu Xi, and the author of the I Ching, and a tradition of classical poetry lasting over millennia, including such names as Li Bai and Wang Wei.

Śāntānanda Sarasvatī said: 'Sanskrit is the conscious language, and all others are distorted, losing their consciousness in course of time'(1965 Day 11). This is a challenging and controversial statement. Evidence for it will be considered in subsequent chapters and include the purity and unchanging nature of sounds in Sanskrit, its reflection of natural laws, and its refinement and order.

It is possible to assess English in this way, using as a start the elements of sound and lawfulness. The sounds are variable, not only in time and geography, but even for the same letter in the same time and place, and there are few principles for maintaining consistency of pronunciation. Lawfulness is not a concept which comes readily to mind for the pronunciation of English, (the nouns 'wind' and 'mind' for example), and the pull of history, based on earlier ways of sounding the language, forces the laws of spelling into incomprehensible complexity at times. Compare the spelling of 'fawn', 'fort', 'fought', 'fraught', and 'floor', and 'feat', 'feet', 'receive', 'retrieve' and 'scene'. These double distortions of sound and spelling can impede the flow of consciousness.

Compared with Sanskrit, and even English, Mandarin has

considerably more irregularity in its sounds. As with English, and possibly more so, due to the absence of an alphabet, these irregularities can cover over qualities associated with consciousness, such as transparency, clarity, and purity. However its grammatical structure is much simpler than that of either English or Sanskrit, and this may provide some explanation for its longevity. It also naturally leads to an aphoristic mode of expression. This has enabled the wisdom of its great teachers to be preserved in succinct statements which remain in common use to this day. Such statements can give an indication of what lies beyond language.

2.8 Reflectivity

In the context of language reflectivity concerns the ability to reflect accurately what is happening at the spiritual, mental and material levels. If there are no words to describe something, subtle or abstract as well as material, then it will be very difficult to recognise and evaluate it. If words confuse different ideas, emotions and values, the society will be the poorer for it.

Sanskrit is rich in concepts and constructions which enable the subtlest levels of the mental and emotional world to be spoken about. It is, of course, also the language in which Advaitic philosophy has been principally expressed. It is noted for its range of spiritual vocabulary. For example, while in English there are the words 'soul', 'spirit' and 'self', and in Mandarin *linghun* and *po*, equivalents in Sanskrit are *ātman, paramātman, adhyātman, jīvātman, puruṣa, aham, jīva, kṣetrajña* and *antaḥkaraṇa*, all distinguishing different meanings. When new words are formed this takes place lawfully, based on *dhātu*s and *pratyaya*s, thus maintaining the integrity of the language at the same time as expanding it. There are many more compound words in Sanskrit than in English or Mandarin, enabling concepts to be expressed in a more succinct and unified way.

English has a very wide range of vocabulary due to the diversity of its sources. This has derived from Anglo-Saxon with its Indo-European source, combined with French, Latin, German and Italian vocabulary, also with an Indo-European source, but via other routes. In the era of the British Empire, it has taken in yet more words from languages in India, Africa, Australia, North America and other countries. The two streams of Anglo-Saxon and French after the Norman Conquest often gave rise to two words for the same thing, which produced subtle differences. Consider, for instance, these pairs of words: end and conclusion, start and commencement, bit and morsel, answer and response, freedom and liberty, wisdom and knowledge. Due to the world-wide expansion of English, its vocabulary is continuing to expand.

In Mandarin, context and tone is very important for understanding meaning, as in the example given earlier of 'ma' having four completely different meanings. As far as vocabulary is concerned, an inward looking attitude in China over the last thousand years may have limited the vocabulary until recently, but like Sanskrit it has a tendency to maintain its integrity by coining new Mandarin words to stand for new foreign concepts, instead of simply importing the foreign word as often happens in English.

2.9 Stability

A living language which has remained stable over the ages, in its spoken, written and grammatical forms, gives cohesion to the culture. The finest literature, the teachings of wise men, the statements of great leaders, can all be easily communicated, despite the different ages in which they arose. If the language itself contains the qualities already described of unity, sound quality, lawfulness, consciousness and reflectivity, then it can also be of great benefit to humanity.

Both Sanskrit and Mandarin have shown great stability, having lasted for well over two thousand years with little change in sound (Sanskrit) or written form (Mandarin) or grammatical principles. Sanskrit has maintained a stability in sound because clear rules of pronunciation were established early, and traditions which follow these rules have continued to be respected to the present day. This is not the case with Mandarin where people from different parts of china cannot understand each other, except in writing. This is quite understandable as the written symbols, originally imposed by imperial decree, bear no consistent relation to sounds, even though various attempts have been made over the centuries to reduce the number of characters and simplify the writing of them. Communication at all levels is hampered by this writing system: printing of books, e-mail messages, learning the language, consistency of pronunciation, difficulty of writing, even simple comprehension of meaning. Although the written forms of Sanskrit have changed over the centuries, the stability of the sounds has meant that the written forms, in whatever system is used, simply translate those sounds into forms, and therefore maintain the stability of the language.

Sanskrit's grammatical structure has also remained substantially unchanged over this period due to the comprehensive nature of the inflectional system established several thousand years ago. Nevertheless, the sheer complexity of the grammar has led to Sanskrit being replaced by derived local languages such as Hindi and Urdu for everyday use. Mandarin has a far simpler grammar, being analytical, and although this has changed somewhat over the centuries, its principles have stayed largely unchanged, and it remains in widespread use.

English, in common with most modern languages, has changed a great deal over the centuries, in sound, grammar and written form. In Anglo-Saxon times, Old English, as it is now known, was a highly inflected language, but over the centuries it has become steadily more analytical, losing most of its inflections. This has the advantage of being simpler for everyone to learn and use, and therefore fitter for the purpose of everyday common usage. As has already been noted, it has also assimilated much new vocabulary from other languages. Although the Roman alphabet was introduced in the ninth century due to the influence of Latin, spelling was not standardised until the sixteenth century, after the introduction of printing. Shortly after this standardisation a number of changes in pronunciation took place, leaving us with a legacy of many words not sounding as they are spelt.

2.10 Summary

From this brief initial comparison, a few tentative conclusions begin to emerge. All languages have three basic aspects, sound, grammar and the ability to communicate, so we will consider each of these in the context of the Advaitic principles of truth explored in this chapter.

When the sounds of the three languages are compared, Sanskrit is clearly the most lawful and stable, and its sounds are reflected most directly in writing. It could therefore be said to have more of the qualities of purity and transparency, which are also qualities of consciousness. Both English and Mandarin in their different ways have variable, changing and inconsistent pronunciation, which do not reflect in the written form. Mandarin is also handicapped by not having a basic set of sounds, an alphabet.

When the grammar of these languages is viewed from these

criteria, the distinction between analytical and inflectional languages comes to the fore. Analytical languages such as Mandarin and, to a lesser extent, English, are easier to use, whereas highly inflected languages, like Sanskrit, convey a greater sense of unity, and the way in which their words are formed can be seen as reflecting formative principles in the natural world. Being formed and held in a far more ordered and structured way, with little scope for common usage to influence and modify its forms, such a language has a more conscious and unchanging quality to it. Although the criterion of stability can work with both types of language, as we have seen with Mandarin writing and Sanskrit sounding, the stability of sound seems to have a far greater value than that of written forms.

The ability of a language to communicate depends on its vocabulary and grammar, and its ease of communication and adaptability to society's needs. However, in the present context we are considering its ability to communicate the truth. English has the most comprehensive vocabulary, Sanskrit has the most developed vocabulary and grammar for conveying spiritual concepts, and Mandarin's strength lies in its grammatical simplicity and scope for aphorisms. English may be easier to communicate than either Mandarin or Sanskrit, but for conveying truth, in the Advaitic sense, Sanskrit appears to be the best equipped. As English is the most widely used language geographically today and also has a long history of effortlessly incorporating words from other languages, there may be some room for useful compromise here, with Sanskrit words being incorporated into English where there is no exact equivalent. We already have guru, yoga, rishi, mantra, and ashram, for example. It would be particularly useful to add *ātman* to this list, as there is no word in English for a soul which is exactly the same in everyone, and identical with God or Brahman.

This chapter contains a number of broad concepts and what may appear sweeping generalisations, but I hope the characteristics of a language which can express truth clearly is beginning to emerge. Subsequent chapters will be more searching in their examination of the evidence for Sanskrit fulfilling this role. Unity and consciousness are addressed in most chapters, sound and stability particularly in chapter 3, and lawfulness in chapters 4 and 7. We will return to the subject again in the concluding chapter, in a wider context.

Note

1. Book 16 of *The Corpus Hermeticum* translated by Clement Salaman, Dorine van Oyen and William D Wharton, Duckworth 1999

Chapter 3

Basic elements of language as evident in Sanskrit

3.1 Setting the scene

Over the next few chapters attention is concentrated on how languages are constituted, with particular reference to the Sanskrit language, and how this may relate to Advaita. The constituents range from alphabets, through grammatically recognised parts of words, words themselves and different types of words, relationships between words, to sentences and finally to meaning.

Modern linguistics, the study of language, addresses all these matters, grouped into three subjects, which themselves each divide into two. It may help to identify what these subjects are called. The three subjects concern sound, structure and meaning, which relate to pronunciation, grammar and semantics respectively. The study of pronunciation divides into phonetics and phonology. Phonetics is the science of speech sounds, especially of their production, transmission and reception, while phonology addresses how sounds are organised to convey words and meaning. The study of grammar divides into morphology and syntax. Morphology relates to word formation and is the study of the smallest meaningful unit of grammar, a morpheme, while syntax relates to word combination and the formation and structure of sentences. The study of semantics divides into lexicology, which addresses vocabulary, and into the analysis of text or discourse.

Linguistics

Sound (Pronunciation)	–	Phonetics and Phonology
Structure (Grammar)	–	Morphology and Syntax
Meaning (Semantics)	–	Lexicology and text/discourse

It is interesting to note that the three Vedāngas, branches of the Veda, most concerned with language have a close affinity with these three areas of linguistics. *Śīkṣā* is pronunciation, *vyākaraṇa* is grammar, and *nirukta* is etymology of words.

This chapter is concerned with pronunciation, and latterly with grammar; chapter 4 is about grammar; chapter 5 about grammar and also semantics; and chapter 6 about semantics.

3.2 The Alphabet

The basic sounds of a language are represented by symbols, often called letters, and collectively, the alphabet. In most languages these sounds do not follow any coherent order, but in Sanskrit there is a very definite, precise and systematic order, related to mouth position and method of articulation. Each of the five principal vowels is sounded in one of five mouth positions: *a* throat , *i* back of palate, *ṛ* roof of mouth , *ḷ* teeth, and *u* lips. They may also all be sounded nasally, and in three time measures, short, long (twice a short measure) and prolonged (more than two measures). There are also four compound vowels, *e ai o* and *au,* each deriving from a pair of vowels. There are 25 consonants, in groups of five, also related to these five mouth positions. Each group of five is distinguished into five methods of articulation: unaspirated, aspirated, unvoiced, voiced, and nasalised. For example the five consonants in the throat position (guttural) are *k* unaspirated and unvoiced, *kh* aspirated and unvoiced, *g* unaspirated and voiced, *gh* aspirated and voiced, and *ṅ* nasal, unaspirated and voiced. There are also four sibilants, *ś ṣ s* and *h*, and four semi-vowels, *y r l* and *v,* all related to specific mouth positions and methods of articulation. (Strictly, we should add an *a* to each of these consonants in order to sound them eg *ka kha).* The existence of such an ordered system of sound provides a stable foundation for the language. Each letter has one sound; so, for example, the letter *a*, unlike in English, is always sounded the same way.

Those are a few facts about the Sanskrit alphabet. Much has been said about the deeper significance of these sounds. One such statement, from Śrī Aurobindo, is: 'Every one of [Sanskrit's] vowels and consonants has a particular and inalienable force, which exists by the nature of things and not by development or human choice: these are the fundamental sounds which lie at the base of the Tantric seed mantras or constitute the efficacy of the mantra itself.' I am not going to write at length on this subject, but here are some fundamental features of these sounds.

3.3 *Mātrikā*

According to Advaita the universe arises from *śabdabrahman* – literally 'Brahman as word' – that word being symbolised by ॐ. The next level of sound is fundamental to the form of the universe and everything in it. This is the level of *mātrikā*, expressed as sixteen sounds, represented as *a ā i ī u ū ṛ ṝ ḷ ḹ e ai o au ṁ aḥ*. The word *mātrikā* can also mean 'mother' and 'source', and derives from the *dhātu mā*, 'measure out' or 'form'. Śāntānanda Sarasvatī describes them as the basic measures which give rise to the forms and qualities of this creation at the causal, subtle and physical levels. They constitute the measures of creation, the natural laws, or the 'will' of the Absolute. These measures regulate creation, being expressed as *śakti* or powers at the subtle level, and *kalā* or great works and qualities at the material level, such as a Shakespeare play or a Mozart concerto.

These sixteen *mātrikās* are reflected in the fourteen vowels of the Sanskrit alphabet, plus two other sounds in that alphabet, a nasal sounded only through the nose, called *anusvāra*, (*ṁ*) and an exhalation of breath called a *visarga* (*ḥ*). Both of these sounds are open sounds like vowels, and do not have the consonantal quality of contact within the vocal apparatus. The words themselves hold a further clue to their inclusion as *mātrikās*. *Anusvāra* literally means 'following a vowel', and in this context can be seen as referring to all the consonants, as these follow the vowels in the alphabet and also cannot be sounded without a vowel (see next paragraph). *Visarga* has many meanings including 'creation' and 'emission', deriving from the *dhātu visṛj*, 'to pour forth, emit', and in this context can be seen as the creative force with which all sounds of the language pour forth in breath.

3.4 Vowels and consonants

Vowels are the basic sounds, not needing any support from another sound for their expression. The Sanskrit word for vowel, *svara*, comes from the *dhātu svṛ* which carries the senses of uttering a sound, singing, praising and shining. The famous Sanskrit grammarian Patañjali, who wrote a commentary on Pāṇini's work about 2,000 years ago, defined a vowel as 'That which shines by itself.' Consonants perform the essential function of supplying a range of breath stops which limit and shape the breath when it is conveying vowels, to enable distinct syllables and words to be formed and expressed. Vowels can be seen as the conscious element in language and consonants as the limiting element. Life and breath are in the vowel sounds; the consonants are subtly different contacts between different parts of the vocal apparatus. There is no contact in vowel sounds, the breath is unimpeded. The combination of vowels and consonants is like the combination of consciousness and matter (*puruṣa* and *prakṛti*) from which creation arises.

Among the vowels, the sound *a*, pronounced with open throat and mouth, is recognised as having a special status. In chapter 10 of the Bhagavad Gītā Krishna says, 'I am the letter *a* of all letters.' In the Aitareya Āraṇyaka there is the statement: '*A* is the entire speech; diversified in association with the consonants, it yet abounds and becomes manifest.' This sound is essential to, and pervades, all sounds in the alphabet. It is simple to recognise in practice as it is sounded with all parts of the vocal apparatus fully open. All other sounds are formed by some modification of this openness.

Much has been said about the qualities of various groups of sounds, but some caution is necessary, as different schools of thought say different things. For example, in one tradition, vowels are feminine as they illuminate themselves, whereas in another they are masculine as they provide the seed, and consonants are feminine as they provide the matrix of language.

3.5 Chakras

There is further evidence for the special character of the sounds of the Sanskrit alphabet. In the Yoga philosophy and in Kashmir Shaivism much is said about the chakras, subtle centres of energy within the body. Each of the chakras is said to hold certain sounds of the Sanskrit alphabet, and together they contain all the sounds. Chakras are wheels, but in relation to the body they are considered as spinning wheels of energy or force, each one associated with a particular gland or organ. They have also been called centres of consciousness. In speech, the sounds of the alphabet are called out from the chakras in much the same way as letter keys on a computer keyboard are struck. When there is a desire, consciousness activates the chakras and the appropriate sounds rise into the mind in a particular order to form an idea.

3.6 The *Māheśvara* Sūtras

In Sanskrit the alphabet is regarded as the substance supporting and pervading grammar. This essential relationship is expressed in fourteen sūtras called the Sūtras of the Great Lord (*Māheśvara*), which set out the letters of the alphabet in fourteen groups. The letters are in a very particular order, related to their natural phonetic affinity with each other through methods of articulation and mouth positions. This order is subtly different from the alphabetic order set out earlier in the chapter. Śāntānanda Sarasvatī has said that in these sūtras and their groupings 'all the laws of grammar are held. [They] then proceed to regulate persons, numbers, genders, conjugations and declensions etc, and produce numerous words and names, which give us the facility to express and communicate all our desires, feelings and deeds together with all things of the world' (Day 4 1974). The significance of this statement is not easy to appreciate until the grammar has been studied for some time.

The classical Sanskrit grammarians, of whom Pāṇini is the most famous, constantly refer to these groups of letters when describing the grammar, showing how the language grows lawfully out of these elements. This is not the usual view of language, where words are regarded as the principal elements. Approaching language from its basic sounds leads to a very different view of what language is. Here, sound is fundamental, whereas meaning arises later; indeed the unity of meaning is only present when a whole sentence has been spoken or read.

These groups of letters are always expressed in classical grammar texts by single syllable words called *pratyāhāras*, thus avoiding the need to refer to all the letters in the group each time. This gives a great succinctness to the statements made by Pāṇini in his descriptive grammar. It may be of interest to note that *pratyāhāra* in a spiritual context is the discipline of withdrawing the mind from external objects in order to be one with the Self.

3.7 *Dhātus* (roots or seeds)

Most words in Sanskrit come from *dhātus*, translated as 'root' or 'seed' of a word. For example, the *dhātu sthā* gives rise to many Sanskrit words. It has the essential meaning of 'stand' and 'stop'. Many English words are cognate with this *dhātu*: stand, station, stable, static, state, establish, stump, standard, statue and constitution, to name but a few of them. The root of the word '*dhātu*' itself is *dhā* and carries senses such as 'put', 'place', 'establish', 'generate', 'create'. Root and seed are somewhat limited translations as they suggest different stages or parts in the development of plants. 'Essential element' gives a closer sense of its meaning and function, although it is not the only essential element in a word.

There are about 2,000 common *dhātus* in Sanskrit, most consisting of single syllable sounds, made up of a vowel and, in most cases, one or two consonants. *Dhātus* are not words, but constitute the first element in the formation of words. Each *dhātu* may give rise to many words, with many meanings, sometimes many hundreds of words, but all derived from their common parent.

3.8 *Pratyayas* (suffixes)

To develop into words, *dhātus* join with *pratyayas*, called suffixes in English, and *upasargas*, or prefixes. However, in Sanskrit the *pratyaya* plays a much more fundamental role than a suffix. Most *dhātus* are monosyllabic, and always require the addition of *pratyayas* to develop into words. The word *pratyaya* is interesting in itself. It comes from the *dhātu i* with the prefix *prati* and has the sense of 'going towards' and also 'returning'. *Pratyaya* has an extraordinary range of meanings in different contexts. It can mean 'belief', 'trust', 'idea', 'consciousness', 'understanding' and 'cause', as well as 'suffix'. The dry technical word 'suffix' may seem rather strange in such company, but the English word clearly has a quite different derivation, to do with fixing to something. When we look for a greater sense of the function and nature of a *pratyaya* by examining its other meanings, we move into new territory. Consciousness, understanding, idea and cause do not at first sight appear to have much connection with suffix, but a closer examination in the light of a wider philosophical view, does bring out some fundamental aspects of the formation of language.

In the Sāṅkhya philosophy – one of six classical Indian philosophical systems – there are two fundamental principles: substance (or nature), *prakṛti*, and the conscious element, *puruṣa*, another word for *ātman* or Self; and the creative process is a combination of these two. In Advaita these two principles are united. Substance is contained within, appears to arise from, is sustained by, and dissolves into, consciousness. In nature, a seed carries its own genetic code, which determines its potential in creation, while the environment in which that seed is located, both physical and subtle, determines how and if that potential is expressed. The seed itself is like a *dhātu*, its environment which provides the action and nourishment is like *pratyaya*, and their combination produces the entity or the word. This is a conscious process, whereas in other languages it is largely unacknowledged.

The same process is reflected in the way Sanskrit grammar describes the growth of a word. The *dhātu* itself is singular, but there are nine different types of *pratyaya*, which can combine with that one *dhātu* to produce many different words, or even new *dhātus*. The *pratyayas* shape the *dhātu* into a noun or a verb, or any of their subcategories, so that one *dhātu* can appear in hundreds, even thousands, of different word forms. Patañjali made a classic statement about *pratyaya*, that 'it makes known, manifests and regulates' the *dhātu*. This power inherent in a *pratyaya* can be seen as an expression of the power inherent in the creative process. That is the conscious principle or *puruṣa* operating in and through the substance or *prakṛti*. That would be an interpretation from the Sāṅkhya view. In Advaita, however, consciousness pervades everything, so the difference between *dhātu*s and *pratyaya*s would be in the different extent to which they reflect and manifest consciousness.

3.9 *Upasarga*s (prefixes)

*Upasarga*s have already been mentioned briefly. There are 22 of them, and when joined to a *dhātu*, they give or suggest a particular direction or redirection to it, or bring out a latent quality of the *dhātu*. This is very similar to English, for example, upset, outset, inset, preset, offset and onset. This element multiplies even more the great number of words which can derive from a particular *dhātu*.

3.10 *Kāraka*s

Another basic element in the formation of Sanskrit words is called *kāraka*. There is no directly equivalent concept in English or indeed in other languages. The definition given in A Dictionary of Sanskrit Grammar by K V Abhyankar and J M Shukla is: 'The capacity in which a thing becomes instrumental in bringing about an action.' A *kāraka* defines the relationship of a word or part of a word to the action being described. These concepts use not only case endings but also several other types of suffixes to indicate their sense. The nearest concept in inflected languages such as Latin and Greek is 'case', but this has a much more limited scope, and is described by another word, *vibhakti*, in Sanskrit. These and other languages can have case endings or prepositions which indicate relationships of words to the action. For example in the sentence: 'He travelled to the station by car', the action is 'travel'. The words 'he', 'station' and 'car' are all related to, and help to shape, this action of travelling. 'He' is agent, 'station' is the object, and 'car' is the means or instrument. These 'cases' are indicated by the actual form of the word 'he', and by the prepositions 'to' and 'by'.

There are six *kāraka*s. These are *kartā* (the actor or agent), *karma* (the object), *karaṇam* (the instrument), *sampradānam* (that to which the action is directed or devoted, its purpose), *apādānam* (the place from which the action comes, its origin), *adhikaraṇam* (the location of the action in time or place). In Latin grammar nominative, accusative, instrumental, dative, ablative and locative bear some relation respectively, but only in certain circumstances. The example sentence already used can be extended to express all the *kārakas*. 'He (*kartā*) travelled from home (*apādānam*) to the station (*karma*) by car (*karaṇam*) in winter (*adhikaraṇam*) for convenience (*sampradānam*). These *kāraka*s can be seen as arising from three pairs. *Kartā* and *karma* express subject and object or cause and effect; *sampradānam* and *apādānam,* the two creative processes of fusion and fission, combination and separation; *karaṇam* and *adhikaraṇam* are both concerned with instrumentality, but *adhikaraṇam* expresses the greatest instrument for this creation, that of time/space.

In the Sanskrit language these *kāraka*s are found not only when expressing relationships between words and action in a sentence, but also in the formation of words themselves.

The most obvious relationships, which have parallels in other inflected languages, are between nouns and the verb of a sentence, as shown in the example sentence 'He travelled to the station by car'. These six relationships are shown by *pratyaya*s applied to the noun, called noun *vibhakti*, which express the particular *kāraka*, the relationship of that word to the verb in the sentence.

Some of these six relationships are also shown by *pratyaya*s called verbal suffixes or *kriyā vibhakti*, which constitute the final part of a verb. They can indicate the *kartā* (giving an active sense) or the *karma* (giving a passive sense).

*Kāraka*s also operate when a *pratyaya* joins with a *dhātu*. These primary *pratyaya*s form stems of words, *prātipadika*s, and often have a *kartā* or agent sense, but there are many examples of other *kāraka* senses. There are examples of this in other languages, such as the 'er' on the end of 'reader', 'waiter', 'teacher' and 'potter', expressing *kartā*.

Suffixes which are joined to the stem (*prātipadika*) of a word to form another stem are called secondary suffixes. An example is the word *saindhava* which means literally ' that which comes from *sindhu*, 'water', and has come to mean 'salt'. Here, the *pratyaya* added to *sindhu* carries the sense of *apādānam*, 'from'.

The final situation is found in expressing relationships between the parts of a compound word, *samāsa*, although here the *kāraka* is usually inferred by context, and not expressed by anything visible in the word.

So at every stage in the development of words, their combination into compound words, and their use in sentences, *kāraka*s are present, always indicating relationship to action. The implications of this will be considered further in the following chapters.

3.11 Number, but not gender

The concept of number in the formation of words is common to most languages, usually to distinguish between singular and plural, in nouns and verbs. Sanskrit also recognises the dual number as a distinct form in declensions and conjugations. In English this distinction is still recognised in words such as 'both', 'pair', 'couple', 'dual', 'double', 'duplicate', 'binary', and 'bi-annual'.

The concept of number as used in language contains both unity and multiplicity. The unity relates to the name of what is being spoken about, such as 'coat' or 'boy'; and the multiplicity relates to one, two or many of that object. In the physical world there will be one, two, or many 'boys', but in language, being in the mental world, there is only one word, the number being indicated by the ending of the word. Pāṇini recognises this distinction between the two worlds by including a sutra which says, 'In place of many (words) of identical form, only one remains when they share the same case.' This recognises the one concept of 'boy' as primary, as it is common to all, while also recognising that multiplicity requires some expression. This is achieved by concentrating on the one concept, but expressing number in the word ending.

Gender is not included in the basic elements of language because it is only a feature of nouns, not verbs, at least in most languages. In Sanskrit one of the three genders is inherent in each noun, sometimes in the form of a feminine suffix, and is expressed in the case endings, which also indicate number and *kāraka*. In English gender remains only in the various forms of the pronouns 'he/she/it' and 'who/what' and the names of certain male and female living beings.

3.12 *Sandhi*

The final element which characterises the formation, and joining, of Sanskrit words is *sandhi*. This is the principle whereby sounds harmonise with each other. The letters in the *Māheśvara* Sutras are grouped according to their common properties of mouth position or means of articulation. Thus all the unvoiced consonants are together, all the semi-vowels are together etc.

There are laws governing how sounds from different groups come together, often causing one letter to change to a particular letter in the group to which the other letter belongs. The word *sandhi* is itself an example, as the final letter of the first part, *sam*, changes to a dental *n* to harmonise with the dental *d* of *dhi*. The laws relating to vowels in juxtaposition are comprehensive. One example of such a law shows how wide-ranging they can be. When an *i, ṛ, ḷ*, or *u* is followed by any other vowel of those four or *a*, it is replaced by *y, r, l*, or *v* respectively, in other words, by its semi-vowel equivalent. For instance, *i* and a following *a* would change to *ya*, and *u* with a following *i* would become *vi*. An example of this is the formation of a word we have already met, *pratyāhāra*, from *prati* and *āhāra*.

This principle of *sandhi* is also evident in other languages, but to a far smaller extent. Here are a couple of English examples: the Latin 'cum', meaning 'with', becomes 'con' in 'conjoin', 'connect', 'contact' and 'consonant', but 'com' in 'communicate', 'combine', 'compact' and 'compile', a difference determined by the mouth position of the following sound; the indefinite article 'a' changes to 'an' in front of another vowel, which is an exact parallel with the negative particle *a* in Sanskrit, which also changes to *an* in front of a vowel.

3.13 Conclusions

The basic elements of the Sanskrit language identified in this chapter are:

1. The alphabet and its expression in chakras and the *Māheśvara* Sutras. The whole language and its grammar arise from these sounds and their order.
2. *Dhātu*, which can be seen as a seed, consisting of a particular combination of letters, waiting to be developed into words.

3. *Pratyaya* or suffix, which makes known, manifests and regulates the *dhātu* to form words through a deliberate, conscious process.
4. *Upasarga* or prefix, the effect of which is to redirect or bring out a latent quality of the *dhātu*.
5. *Kāraka*, which is the relationship of suffixes and words to the action being described (see also chapter 5.4 and 7.4).
6. Number, which in language contains both unity and multiplicity.
7. *Sandhi*, which governs how sounds harmonise (see also chapter 5.5 and App.2)

Although this chapter has concentrated on how these basic elements of language apply in Sanskrit, they are of course present in other languages. The extent to which they are consciously evident is, however, significantly less than in Sanskrit. English, for example, being an Indo-European language, exhibits most of these elements, although much less clearly than in Sanskrit. It has an alphabet of vowels and consonants; words have seed forms and suffixes, although only suffixes are explicitly recognised in its grammar; *kāraka*s are expressed through prepositions, suffixes and word order; number is found in singular and plural; and *sandhi* can be seen in the spelling of some words, but rarely between words.

Unless a language is built on firm and lawful foundations and conscious principles, it will have difficulty in reflecting and communicating clearly and without distortion at all levels, be they material, mental or spiritual. This chapter provides some evidence for Sanskrit meeting this requirement.

Chapter 4

Words: their formation and classes

4.1 In chapter 1 I referred to the universe beginning with the Word, with ॐ, with the Big Bang, and to the continuing and pervasive nature of that beginning. In Advaita that is described as the eternal word which encompasses everything. The use of 'word' suggests that there must be some relation with ordinary words, some essential characteristic which they both share. All words are sound, and sound is vibration. All creation at the material level can be understood as vibrations expressed as electro-magnetic waves, light, infra-red light, X-rays, sound and so on. At this level some relationship between the initial impulse or explosion of energy and the universe as we experience it, can be deduced. But that does not directly help to identify relationships between words in the mental world of language and the original word, ॐ.

Bhartṛhari, the 5th century language philosopher, described words arising from a flash of consciousness called a *sphoṭa*, literally, 'an explosion in consciousness'. In Canto 1 of the Vākyapadīya he distinguishes the eternal from the temporal word. In verse 130 he says

> 'It has been said that the Self, which is within the speaker, is the word.'

In his own commentary on this verse he says

> 'Here (in the science of grammar) the word is of two kinds. It is eternal and it is a product. The product is

> that which is found in worldly usage and it bears the reflection of the Self which is essentially the word. The eternal one is the source of all usage, it has all sequence suppressed, it resides within everybody, the source of all transformations, the substratum of all actions, the basis of pleasure and pain, unimpeded anywhere with regard to the production of effects, (but) with its field of enjoyment restricted like a lamp covered with a jar, the limitless source of all corporeal objects, manifesting itself as all forms of knowledge and as all differentiations.' [1]

Words are mostly considered in their second sense, as a product, in this book, but in Advaita philosophy such words are seen as reflecting the eternal word, which is the Self, and that theme is taken up in this chapter.

4.2 Are words fixed or fluid?

We tend to see words as fixed points in the ever-changing activity of language. They are fixed in that we see them having a defined and limited meaning which is described nowadays in dictionaries. This impression is reinforced in uninflected languages where the form of words changes little, whatever part they may be playing in a sentence. Although sentences are composed of words, they are definitely not fixed. Apart from standard items like greetings, sentences are infinitely variable. For example, each sentence in this book is likely to be unique, both in form and meaning. This fluidity of sentences is also shown in the meaning of words when they are in a sentence. The context of the sentence will greatly affect their meaning. Their existence outside sentences has a certain artificiality, rather like

1 *The Vākyapadīya of Bhartrrhari*, trans and notes Iyer K.A.S., Motilal Banarsidass. 1977

considering parts of a living body separately from the body. A similar view can be taken of the letters of the alphabet which form words with meaning, but in themselves have no meaning.

The extent to which a language is inflected has a direct relation to the degree of fixity or fluidity of its word forms. English has some inflections but very few compared with Sanskrit. For example, in English, 'word' has only three forms – 'word', 'words' and 'word's' – whereas in Sanskrit there are seventeen forms of its equivalent – *pada*. The situation is similar with verbs. In English, the present tense of the verb 'go' only has two forms – 'go' and 'goes'– whereas in Sanskrit there are nine forms of *gam*. This difference changes the very concept of what a word is. In Sanskrit grammar a *pada* is defined as an inflected nominal or verbal expression in a sentence. Before a noun is inflected and goes into a sentence it is called a *prātipadika*, the stem form of the word. Verbs do not have a stem form, as they are far more fluid in their whole formation, the only constant being the *dhātu*. Words in Sanskrit only exist as words once they are playing a part in a sentence, and therefore have nominal and verbal endings. This gives a very different sense to the concept of word, one which is much more fluid, as it is inseparable from the part it is playing in the fluid sentence, except when it is being analysed. Fluidity and change are basic characteristics of the universe.

4.3 The composition of words

Besides inflections, words are composed of other elements, and those explicitly recognised in Sanskrit are set out in the previous chapter. *Dhātu*s, prefixes (*upasarga*s) and suffixes (*pratyaya*s) play fundamental parts in forming words, and contribute their own meanings to the forming word. Normally in modern languages these elements are taken very much for granted, and consequently our understanding of words relates to the whole word, with no acknowledgement of the meanings of its parts. Thus 'understand' is appreciated in its wholeness, without any sense that it is composed of the prefix 'under' and the verb 'stand'. The 22 prefixes (*upasargas*) in Sanskrit are used much more frequently than their equivalents in other languages, and *pratyayas* (suffixes) play a much greater and more consciously explicit role. There are nine different types of *pratyaya*, and hundreds of distinct *pratyayas*. Most words will contain several *pratyayas*, whereas in English they often have none at all, and rarely more than two. This affects the shape of sentences and the number of words used. In the first paragraph of this chapter for instance, there are 137 words. If this were translated into Sanskrit there would be about half this number, due to the much greater use of inflections and suffixes.

The other main element in the formation of words is the *dhātu*, seed or root. Each *dhātu* may give rise to hundreds or even thousands of words. In themselves *dhātus* do have meaning, but more in the sense of the sphere or area in which their meaning or activity is found. A classical work called the *Dhātupāṭha*, in which all *dhātus* are listed, indicates for each *dhātu* a meaning or meanings expressed in the locative case. In other words, the meaning may be found in the concepts or activities indicated, but not on a one to one equivalent basis as in a dictionary. This is not at all surprising as *dhātus* are not words.

A *dhātu* in itself does nothing. It holds a code rather like a blueprint or genetic code, which is then shaped and developed by *pratyayas*. They fuse with and breathe life into it, until the combined expression becomes a fully formed word or *pada*, playing its part in a sentence. This has some parallel with the formation of any living thing. A particular oak tree will have originated from an acorn, just as a word originates from a *dhātu*. The *dhātu* determines that whatever word comes from it will always have as its basis that *dhātu*, just as all trees coming from acorns will be oak trees. When the situation is propitious the acorn will sprout, assimilating nourishment from its environment, and growing into a fully formed tree. This tree is a combination of acorn, encompassing the genetic code for oak contained in it, and elements in the immediate environment. Similarly, when the situation is propitious for a *dhātu* to sprout i.e. when someone wants to speak about something or some activity, the word for which derives from this *dhātu*, it will combine with *pratyaya*s to become the word for that thing or activity. This word is a combination of *dhātu*, including the grammatical laws and meaning contained in the *dhātu*, and relevant *pratyaya*s with their grammatical laws and meanings. Thus, the way words are developed can be seen as a reflection of the natural laws governing the way living beings develop. There is a further stage in this comparison. A living being is always living and moving in a particular time and place, otherwise it would not exist. A word can be seen as only coming into existence as a living word when it is playing a part in a sentence and has a suffix or preposition which signifies this part.

4.4 Examples of forming a word in Sanskrit

To bring home the fact that a Sanskrit word is formed with grammatical laws charting every step of its formation, here are a couple of examples. The description is inevitably somewhat technical, and those who prefer to stay with the main theme, and not go into the detail with its grammatical terms, may cheerfully choose to move on and miss this section.

Formation of a Verb

'I become' is expressed as one word, *bhavāmi*

1. This starts life as the *dhātu bhū* which according to the *Dhātupāṭha* is found 'in being'. This *dhātu* belongs to the first of the ten classes of *dhātu*s, and it therefore conjugates in ways specific to that class, as set out in Pāṇini's sutras. This is rather like the genetic code of the acorn. **bhū**

2. Fundamental to the formation of a verb is a type of *pratyaya* called a *kriyā vibhakti*. The nearest English translation is 'verbal ending'. These endings pack an enormous amount of meaning, including tense, mood, number, grammatical person, *kāraka* and voice. There are only 18 of these *pratyaya*s. How such a small number can convey so many meanings without ambiguity is a subject for another day. The particular *vibhakti* which expresses 'I' in present tense active voice is *mip*. It also expresses the *kartā kāraka* (agent). **mip**

3. This *pratyaya mip* has a special letter *p*, which is an example of a major feature of Pāṇinian grammar, *it* letters, or indicatory letters. These often form part of basic elements of the language such as *dhātu*s and *pratyaya*s, and serve to indicate something. This *p* in *mip* indicates that it will on defined occasions cause certain changes in the form of the *dhātu* to which *mip* is joined. As those occasions are not present in this example we need not investigate further, apart from noting a general feature of all *it* letters; they

are invisible when the element they are attached to becomes part of a word. **bhū + mip**

4. Having established the two basic parts of the verb, its *dhātu* and its *kriyā vibhakti* (verbal affix), we find the next step arising from information contained in those two elements. As *bhū* is in the first class of *dhātu*s and as *mip* is a *kriyā vibhakti* expressing the active voice or *kartā* in the present tense, a further type of *pratyaya* comes in between *bhū* and *mip*. This is called a *vikaraṇa pratyaya* which modifies the form of the *dhātu*. The particular one here is *śap* which contains two *it* letters, *ś* and *p*. These become invisible when *śap* joins with *bhū*, leaving just *a*. **bhū+śap+mip**

   bhū+ a + mi

5. The entry of *śap* has an effect on the *dhātu bhū*, causing the *u* of *bhū* to be replaced by *o*, which is called the *guṇa* form of *u*. **bho + a +mi**

6. The laws of *sandhi*, which govern how sounds change when they come together, are pervasive in Sanskrit. One operates when *o* and *a* come together, and *o* is replaced by *av* before the *a* to give *ava*. **bhava + mi**

7. There is one further step in the formation of this word. When certain *kriyā pratyayas* begin with certain letters, such as *m* in *mip*, they cause a preceding short *a* to lengthen into *ā*. Hence *bhavā*, and the final form of the word is *bhavāmi*. **bhavāmi**

Formation of a Noun

'In Rāma' is expressed as *Rāme*

1. The *dhātu* here is *ram* which is found 'in playing, delighting, stopping and resting'. Information about its class is not relevant here as a noun is being formed, not a verb. **ram**

2. The first *pratyaya* to be added is of a type called *kṛt*, or primary suffix, as they always join directly with the *dhātu*. The particular *pratyaya* here is *ghañ* which has two *it* letters, *gh* and *ñ*. It is added to a *dhātu* when the word being formed is masculine and is related to the *dhātu*'s activity as an instrument or location, another example of *kāraka*. So the word *Rāma* is the instrument or location of delight or rest. i.e. the one in whom or by whom there is delight or rest. **ram + ghañ**

3. The *it ñ* in *ghañ* is indicating that the *a* in *ram* is to be lengthened to *ā*. This, together with the *a* in *ghañ,* forms *Rāma* which is the *prātipadika* or stem form of the word. **Rāma**

4. For this stem to become a *pada*, a fully formed word, another type of *pratyaya* has to be added, called a *nāmavibhakti* or case ending. This expresses the *kāraka* of the word in the sentence, which here is *adhikaraṇa* or locative. In Sanskrit there are twenty one of these case endings because there are seven cases and three numbers, singular, dual and plural. Here the locative singular is expressed by the *nāmavibhakti ṅi*. As *ṅ* is an *it* letter, we are left with *i*. **Rāma + i**

5. Finally a law of *sandhi* now operates as two vowels, *a* and *i*, are next to each other. These two are replaced by the one vowel *e*. **Rāme**

As well as demonstrating the lawful development of words, these examples also show the important role of invisible letters in forming the words, the pervasiveness of the *a* sound, and the principles of *kāraka* and *sandhi*.

4.5 Different classes of word

Words have different grammatical functions and are classified according to these functions. The two classes most commonly cited are nouns and verbs, describing entities and activities, but most modern languages recognise eight classes of word: noun, verb, pronoun, adjective, adverb, preposition, conjunction, and interjection. In the Sanskrit tradition there are four main classes: *nāma* (noun), *kriyā* (verb), *upasarga* (prefix), and *nipāta* (particle). *Nāma* has the subcategories of pronoun and adjective, *kriyā,* of adverb and a whole range of tenses, moods and voices, and *nipāta,* of preposition, conjunction and interjection. The nearest equivalent category to *upasarga* in English is prefix, which is not a separate word. However in Sanskrit this category is treated as a separate word, although it is most often found joined with another word just like a prefix.

Sanskrit grammarians use words for these grammatical functions which show how they are interconnected. One such grammarian was Yaska who lived before Pāṇini and composed a famous treatise on *nirukta* (etymology). He used the word *sattva*, 'substance', for noun, and *bhāva*, 'becoming', for verb. *Sattva* is composed of *sat,* meaning 'being', as it is the present participle of the *dhātu as*, 'to be', while the suffix *tva* gives the sense of substance or nature, like 'ness' in English. 'Beingness' would be a literal translation of *sattva*. *Bhāva* is from the *dhātu* *bhū* 'to become', and has the sense of 'becoming'. The two *dhātus* *as* and *bhū* have very close links. In the *Dhātupāṭha, as* is described as 'in becoming' and *bhū* is described as 'in being'. Also, the future tense of *as* uses the forms of *bhū* . This is helpful in showing that nouns and verbs are essentially two aspects of one activity. Verbs portray particular activities and constitute the centre of a sentence, while nouns are related to the verb, and help to fulfil it. Both are necessary for each other. Activities don't exist without entities, nor entities without activities. How the interrelationship is treated in Sanskrit will be described in the next chapter, on sentences.

The next few paragraphs use a number of grammatical terms but are not intended to be a grammar lesson; instead their purpose here is to point out some aspects of the grammar of words which indicate a deeper significance related to natural law.

4.6 The Verb family

We start from the Advaitic principle that the process of creation is a process of manifestation of the unity, appearing as differentiation from unity into multiplicity. Verbs can reflect and describe this process very fully, particularly in Sanskrit. In developing from *dhātus*, they differentiate in many ways in order to express how activity is manifested. The word *kriyā* itself, deriving from the *dhātu kṛ* meaning 'act', 'do', 'make', has the wider meanings of 'activity', 'action', 'performance' as well as the sense in grammar of a verb.

The first differentiation of verbs is into three persons. They are described as the first person ('he', 'she', 'it' or 'they'), middle ('you') and best ('I' or 'we') in Sanskrit, which equate with third, second and first persons respectively in Western languages.

These three grammatical persons reflect the one person in its three guises, the universal, the one in front, and the one within. In the Advaitic tradition the first person represents *Brahman*, the middle person represents the teacher, and the best person the *Ātman* or Self. The word used for 'person' is *puruṣa,* which is interesting as it also means the Self (see chapter 3.8).

With person comes number: singular, dual and plural, again threefold. The verb also differentiates into three times: past, present and future. There are three voices in Sanskrit. In addition to active and passive, there is also *bhāva*, which simply expresses the activity itself. There is no equivalent form in English, the nearest in translation being expressions like 'there is ruling', 'there is swimming'.

At this point it is worth noting that all the ways so far considered in which activity is expressed and differentiated in language are threefold. There are three persons, three numbers, three times and three voices. This could be seen as an aspect of the law of three, as originally expressed in the movement from one to three, described in the Advaitic concept of the three *guṇ as* or qualities, and the Christian concept of the Trinity.

Verbs also have a number of modes or moods including imperative, interrogative, benedictive (blessing) and conditional. They have special senses such as repetitive, intensive, desiderative, causative and reflexive. All these different ways of describing activity are expressed in different forms of the one verb, each form being a special development of the original *dhātu*, while remaining as one word.

4.7 The Noun family

The Sanskrit word translated as 'noun' is *nāma,* which has a more fundamental meaning, 'name'. The unity of the universe is expressed in the word ॐ from which everything is said to arise as 'name and form only', *nāmarūpaiva*. This is evident in created objects. A gold ring exists in name and form only. If it is melted down, it no longer exists, but the element gold, out of which it is made, does remain. Nouns reflect this principle. Essentially they are made of the elements of language, the sounds of the alphabet, coming together in particular combinations as names or nouns, which in Sanskrit then differentiate into three genders, three numbers and seven sets of case endings called *vibhakti*. Every noun therefore has at least twenty one forms, and, if it appears in all three genders, sixty three forms.

The words used for pronoun (*sarvanāma*) and adjective (*viśeṣaṇa*) in Sanskrit also show their links with the unity. *Sarvanāma* is composed of two elements, *sarva* meaning 'all', and *nāma*, a name or noun. So *sarvanāma* is a name of all, a name that applies to everyone and everything, such as I, you, they, what, that. He, she and it in Sanskrit are all essentially the same word, *tat,* which declines differently in each gender. There is a finite list of *sarvanāma*s and it is rather more extensive than the list of pronouns. It covers words like *sarva* itself, north, south, east and west, left and right, other, first, one, two (but not three onwards). All these words can be seen as applying to everything. This is a quite different understanding from that contained in the English word 'pronoun', 'that which stands for a noun'. A pronoun is merely a replacement term, whereas the equivalent word in Sanskrit represents those nouns which are universal in application.

Viśeṣaṇa is composed of the *upasarga vi* carrying the sense of expansion and differentiation, the noun *śeṣa* which means 'remainder', and the *pratyaya ana*, 'the act of'. Literally *viśeṣaṇa* is 'the act of expanding the remainder'. In Advaita that which always remains is the Absolute, *Brahman*, the Self. It is always present. The function of a *viśeṣaṇa* is to express a particular quality of that which remains, a completely different sense from 'adjective' which literally means 'that which is thrown at something'. Leon MacLaren, speaking in a lecture in 1980, said: 'The English concept of an adjective is you pick up an adjective and you sling it at somebody and it sticks to them. And *viśeṣaṇa*, the concept is wholly different, it is to bring forward a hidden quality of the Absolute and make it manifest. Well, if you address people like that, how different it is. In the simplest possible example which always works, all I have to say to you is: Happy? What is the answer? [Audience response: Yes!]'

There is one further class of noun, not so far mentioned. This is a *samāsa* or compound word. There are compound words in English, such as 'blackbird', which has a different meaning from 'black bird', but in Sanskrit they are far commoner, and are often created just for a particular circumstance. The word *samāsa* comes from a *dhātu* meaning to combine, and it enables one idea to be expressed as a unity, instead of through a number of separate words. This may not sound very significant on the surface, but it does change the understanding at a deep level. For example, in chapter 10 verse 20 of the Bhagavad Gītā there is a sentence of three words: *aham ātmā sarvabhūtāśayasthitaḥ*. This has been translated as 'I am the Self seated in the heart of all beings'. 'I am the Self' is *aham ātmā* and the rest of the sentence is expressed by a *samāsa* consisting of four parts, *sthita* (seated), *āśaya* (in the heart), *sarva bhūta* (of all beings). This concentrated form gives a unified sense which is not so evident in the seven separate English words.

4.8 The unfolding of creation in language

All creation is viewed in Advaita philosophy as one activity. In language, verbs express activity and nouns express a limit on that activity so that it appears to be fixed in a form with a name.

Drawing on Patañjali and Bhartṛhari, a number of levels appear in the expression of this one creative activity.

1. The one activity which is 'being', *sat*. This is beyond language. Everything in the universe partakes of 'being', otherwise it would not exist.
2. A particular activity such as cooking. This is expressed by the *dhātu*.
3. The process of that particular activity, involving agents such as time, person and number. This is expressed by the verb, the *kriyā*, with its tenses and moods, and its *vibhakti* endings, giving person, number and active, passive or *bhāva* voice.
4. Finally, those agents of the activity which are expressed separately from the verb are nouns or nominal phrases in the sentence, having relationships to the verb, and aiding its accomplishment (or non-accomplishment). Bhartṛhari says that nouns have powers and these powers are expressed by the *kāraka*s, the relationships with the verb.

4.9 Fluidity between classes of word

The distinction between nouns and verbs is not as fixed as the above description might lead one to think. To start with they share many common characteristics, certainly in Sanskrit. The *dhātu* is common to both; they may both have prefixes, *upasarga*s; both are formed with *pratyaya*s, although with different types of *pratyaya*; both end with *vibhakti pratyaya*s, although again with different ones; and they both express *kāraka*s. In practice, some participles may act as main verbs while being formed like a noun. For example, in the sentence: 'The soldier is killed', the Sanskrit equivalent could be just two words: *Sainikaḥ* <u>*hataḥ*</u> where the participle *hataḥ* is translated as 'is killed'. Similarly, 'that is to be done' is *tat kartavyam*. In an active sentence, 'He went to the wood' Sanskrit still has the choice of expressing this with a participle, *sa vanam gatavān* or a verb, *sa vanam agacchat*. Present participles such as 'going' are formed with both nominal and verbal *pratyaya*s, and therefore in Sanskrit have both nominal and verbal characteristics.

There is also a fluidity between nouns and adjectives in Sanskrit. Both may share the same form, and only the context and specific gender will make clear which role the word is playing. In the Monier-Williams Sanskrit-English dictionary the noun/adjective will appear under one entry, the grammatical distinction being apparent only because the English adjectival meanings will be prefaced by *mfn* indicating that all genders are applicable, while the noun meanings will be prefaced by one gender.

This fluidity runs right through the Sanskrit language, deriving from the emphasis on *dhātu*s rather than on words as the basis of the language. Words are much more fluid in both role and form in Sanskrit, and can have many meanings.

4.10 The word *Saṁskṛta*

To conclude this short exploration of word formation and classes of word, it is worth examining the word *Saṁskṛta* itself (spelt 'Sanskrit' in English) to see what this shows. It is comprised of the prefix *sam* with the senses of 'complete', 'whole', 'perfect', and the past participle *kṛta* with the senses of 'formed' 'made' 'prepared' (the change from *m* to *ṁs* is a *sandhi* change). The *dhātu* is *sam-kṛ* meaning 'to make perfect, to form well, to refine,' and the literal translation of *Saṁskṛta* is 'well or completely formed or perfected'. As a noun, it means a word formed accurately according to rules, and has come to mean the whole language. On this basis, a word can be examined to see whether it is a Sanskrit word or not. The practice of taking in a word from another language and using it with only minor changes is not possible in Sanskrit. A new idea expressed by a foreign word would have to be understood first, and then a Sanskrit word created based on an appropriate *dhātu* joining with appropriate *pratyaya*s.

4.11 Word and words again

In this exploration of words, particularly in the Sanskrit language, the reflective link, mentioned at the beginning of this chapter, between the eternal Word and words in human languages, can be seen in a variety of ways. The fluidity of words, the lawful way in which they are formed, the relation of nouns and verbs to each other and to the one activity of creation, the names given to particular classes of word in Sanskrit, and the frequent use of compound words, all strengthen this recognition. There are other ways, such as the four stages of speech, *parā*, *paśyantī*, *madhyamā*, and *vaikharī*, which demonstrate the movement from unmanifest to manifest. This subject will be considered in the next chapter as it relates more particularly to sentences.

Chapter 5

Sentences and relationships within them

5.1 What is a sentence?

Having considered the elements of a word, and words themselves, we now come to combinations of words into a unit of speech, that is, a sentence. Sentences can consist of one word as well as many words, so what distinguishes a sentence from a word? A dictionary definition of sentence is 'meaningful linguistic unit, i.e. a group of words or a single word that expresses a complete thought, feeling or idea.' It has been argued that a sentence must contain a verb, or an implied verb. That is based on the principle that a meaningful linguistic unit must contain an activity, even if that activity is simply being or existing. Every sentence in this book will contain a verb, or an implied verb. 'Happy Birthday', and 'Yes' are sentences. Even 'Happy Birthday' implies 'I wish you a Happy Birthday', and 'Yes' implies agreement with what someone has just said.

5.2 Sentence as a unity

Bhartṛhari argued that the sentence was the indivisible unit of communication, expressing a unity, which individual words did not, and that it alone was real and fit for communication. Before the sentence is spoken it is already a unity, an internal unity, and after expression it is an external unity. Initially, in its conceptual stage, the sentence is called a *sphoṭa*, a flash of consciousness, which expands in the mind of the speaker and is finally expressed in speech. When it is heard by the hearer there is a corresponding flash of understanding called *pratibhā*, and the meaning is appreciated. In both instances the sentence is whole and indivisible. To explain this indivisible unity he compared a sentence with a portrait. Although it is possible to identify different colours and features in the portrait, their plurality does not affect the unity of the portrait as a whole, and that is what is appreciated by both the speaker/painter and the hearer/viewer. Wittgenstein also regarded the sentence as the basic functional unit of language, not the word. He showed that words can only be understood when they are spoken in a particular sentence in a particular situation.

When a word is regarded as an individual independent unit, this appears to rest on a view of creation consisting of multiple things and activities. The basis is multiplicity, whereas, when the sentence is seen as the smallest unit, the basis is the essential unity of the many. The sentence is a complete activity and this complete unit reflects an aspect of the one activity, which is the whole of creation. A word could be a noun, a verb, a particle, a qualifier (adjective or adverb), or a compound word making up a phrase. A sentence is not the sum of the words in it, as it conveys a meaning over and above the words. In inflected languages like Sanskrit there is a further argument in favour of the sentence as the unit. When there are inflections, the word adopts a different form according to the role it is playing in the particular sentence, so it is very obvious that the word cannot be appreciated apart from the context of that sentence along with the other words in the sentence. Even in analytical languages where words appear to remain separate, this is not really the case, as the word is often part of a phrase, such as 'on the tree', 'have been sleeping', 'to be done', and only makes full sense in the complete phrase, or rather, the complete sentence. The order of the words in the sentence is also crucial to its meaning.

Acceptance of the sentence as the unit of communication

and understanding does not negate the value of analysing the sentence into its component words and phrases and their relationships, or of analysing words themselves. However, such exercises then become secondary activities, not the primary one, which is to understand the sentence as a whole.

5.3 Formation of a Sentence

Describing how a word is formed is a somewhat artificial exercise concerned with grammatical concepts such as *dhātu*s and *pratyaya*s. Describing how a sentence is formed is rather different, if one accepts that a sentence is the basic meaningful unit of speech. To the speaker the sentence is already there as a unity in mind before it is spoken. Development from this initial stage to the fully formed sentence spoken aloud is described by Advaitic teachers as having four identifiable stages, called *parā*, *paśyantī*, *madhyamā*, and *vaikharī*.

The first stage, *parā*, is hardly a stage at all, being described by Śāntānanda Sarasvatī as 'pure consciousness in knowledge and substance.' It is still and beyond normal experience. *Parā* literally means 'beyond' and is expressed in the feminine because it is describing speech, a feminine word in Sanskrit. However, from the individual's perspective it has a location in the body, the navel. All speech starts from there, but it has no form at that level.

The second stage is called *paśyantī*. Śāntānanda Sarasvatī describes this stage as 'the poised state of action. In this state the mind and the *prāṇa*s are joined together and vibrations manifest.' He likens it to standing at a crossroads with everything under observation. The word itself is the present participle of the verb 'to see' and therefore literally means 'seeing'. Like *parā*, *madhyamā*, and *vaikharī* it is expressed in the feminine gender. At this stage the whole sentence is in its causal state as a *sphoṭa*.

This interesting concept of *sphoṭa* warrants a slight diversion here to explore its meaning and significance. It appears to have originated with Patañjali who defined it as 'the eternal and imperceptible element of sounds and words, and the real vehicle of the idea which bursts or flashes on the mind when a sound is uttered.' Leon MacLaren referred to it as 'an explosion in consciousness', 'a creative desire'. He spoke of it as holding cause, action and effect, and the law governing these. Bhartṛhari developed the concept identified by Patañjali very fully and identified these characteristics:

a) indivisible unity, over and above sounds;
b) primarily manifested in sentence, only secondarily in word;
c) conveys meaning, sentence being the primary meaningful unit;
d) permanent; manifested, not produced;
e) has no sequence, whereas sounds and letters do.

Sphoṭa could be applied to more than just a sentence; it could relate to a speech, a whole life and has even been referred to by Swāmi Vivekānanda in the following words:

'The eternal *Sphoṭa*, the essential, eternal, material of all ideas or names, is the power through which the Lord creates the Universe. *Sphoṭa* has one word as its only possible symbol, and this is ॐ. *Sphoṭa* is the material of all words. If all peculiarities which distinguish words from each other, be removed, then what remains is *Sphoṭa*.'

It has to be said that Shankara argued against the existence of *sphoṭa* in his commentary on the Brahma Sutras (Book 1.3.8), on the grounds that to appreciate the meaning of a word it was only necessary to hear the letters forming the words and their order. To introduce the additional concept of *sphoṭa* into this appreciation was 'unnecessary and fanciful'. It appears from a reading of the discussion that a different meaning of the word *sphoṭa* is understood here, one relating to appreciation of meaning and not to expression of speech.

Be that as it may, if we take *sphoṭa* as concerned with expression by the speaker rather than appreciation of meaning by the hearer, it can be seen as having direct significance in the manifestation of speech, and in that context is associated with *paśyantī*. The location of this stage is the heart/chest area.

When one of the possibilities at the crossroads of *paśyantī* has been chosen by the speaker, the sound of that possibility rises in his or her mental world, and this is called *madhyamā* – the middle stage. This stage, located in the area between the chest and the throat, is where the sentence takes shape, drawing on the letters of the alphabet, said to be held in the chakras. Here the sentence is objectified insofar as it comes into the field of vision of the speaker, whereas at the *paśyantī* stage the sentence is still united with the speaker or observer. Finally the sentence is spoken using the vocal apparatus of tongue etc, and this stage, when the sound is physically evident, is called *vaikharī*. Here the articulation is elaborated, and includes the characteristic sound of the individual.

It should now be clearer why this fourfold stage of speech is related directly to the sentence and not to the word. The unit of speech is the sentence, not the word. Sentences are conceived as a whole, as a *sphoṭa*, and brought into spoken sound, using individual words, but the words are not themselves conceived separately. They are an integral part of the sentence.

5.4 Relationships within a sentence

When a sentence is seen as the basic unit of communication and understanding, relationships within a sentence become most important in understanding its meaning. The principal relationships are between entities (nouns) and activity (verb), the activity being described by the sentence, and these relationships are expressed through the *kāraka*s. Indeed one translation of the word *kāraka* is 'relation to the activity'. These have been mentioned before in chapters 3.10 and 4.4 with their six names, *kartā* etc. In a sentence *kartā* is the agent or nominative, *karma* the object or accusative, *karaṇam* instrumental, *sampradānam* dative, *apādānam* ablative and *adhikaraṇam* locative. They are expressed by noun case suffixes and by verbal suffixes. These share a common name of *vibhakti pratyaya*. The noun *vibhakti pratyaya*s (case endings) express all of the *kāraka*s. The verbal *vibhakti pratyaya*s express only *kartā* or *karma*, which in Western grammars are described as active and passive voices.

The centre of any sentence is its activity, expressed by a verb, either explicitly or implicitly. All other words are defined by their relationship to the activity. They are there as agents for the accomplishment of the activity and play various roles to that end, the six principal roles being expressed through the *kāraka*s. This can be represented by the analogy of a circle with the activity at the centre and each radius being one of the *kāraka*s. There are several interesting points to note about how this key concept in Sanskrit grammar applies in a sentence.

All six *kāraka*s are agents (*kartā*) helping to accomplish the action, but only one gets that name. This is the principal agent, the one which is independent of the others and in effect organises the others to fulfil their agent roles. The other five are subsidiary agents, independent within their own sphere, but controlled overall by the principal agent.

Take the sentence, 'The artist drew the girl's portrait from a photo with a pencil in the garden.' 'Artist' is clearly the principal agent of the activity of drawing, but portrait, photo, pencil and garden are also agents. Without a pencil, photo, garden and her portrait, the activity expressed by the sentence would not be complete, yet they are all dependent on the artist.

There are seven noun *vibhakti*s but only six *kāraka*s. This gives the first hint that the two concepts are not related on a one to one basis. The first and sixth noun *vibhakti*s are not related directly to *kāraka*s in the system set out by Pāṇini. However the other five are. The second expresses *karma*, the third *karaṇam* and *kartā,* the fourth *sampradānam*, the fifth *apādānam*, and the seventh *adhikaraṇam*.

The sixth expresses a relationship between nouns, the genitive case in Western grammar, not between a noun and the activity of the sentence; hence it cannot be called a *kāraka*. The word ' girl's ' in the example sentence just given would be expressed by the sixth *vibhakti*. Here, the girl is not directly related to the activity of the sentence (drawing) but to the portrait, which is not an activity.

The reason why no *kāraka* is expressed by the first *vibhakti* is much subtler, and may be based on the Advaitic principle that the Self does not act. Pāṇini states that *kartā*, the principal agent, is expressed by nine of the eighteen verbal *vibhakti*s (these are called *parasmaipada*) and by the third noun *vibhakti*. *Karma* may be expressed by the other nine verbal *vibhakti*s (called *ātmanepada*) and by the second noun *vibhakti*. The interesting point here is that the first noun *vibhakti*, which one would automatically expect to represent the *kartā*, is limited by Pāṇini simply to naming, and has no *kāraka* role. When the verb is in the active voice, the *kartā* will be expressed by the verbal *vibhakti*, so in *gacchati* (he, she or it goes) the *vibhakti ti* at the end of *gacchati* expresses the *kartā*. But we usually give a name to the *kartā*, such as 'the man goes', and here in Sanskrit, 'man', *nara,* would have a first noun *vibhakti*, becoming *naraḥ*, which would name the *kartā* expressed in the verb. This naming sense may be the origin of the Western grammatical term 'nominative', that which nominates. In expressing a passive activity such as *annam khādyate* (the food is eaten), the verbal *vibhakti* would change from *ti* to *te* to express the *karma*. *Anna* as the name of the *karma* would be in first noun *vibhakti*. In this second sentence there may still be a *kartā*, but not being the principal focus of the sentence, and therefore not expressed in the verb, this *kartā* would be in the third noun *vibhakti* – *annam nareṇa khādyate* ('the food is eaten by the man'). This distinction between *kāraka* and *vibhakti* has an affinity with the modern concepts of deep and surface grammar (see chapter 1.5), with *kāraka* expressing the former and *vibhakti* the latter.

The philosophical import of these distinctions goes to the heart of Advaita teaching. In chapter 5 of the Bhagavad Gītā there is the famous statement " 'I do nothing at all' so does the wise man think." At the centre of any action there is no 'doer', no agent, although in the world of multiplicity there certainly appears to be one. The centre of any action when expressed in speech is the verb, so in an active sentence any sense of 'doership' would naturally be integral to and non-different from the verb, and in a passive sentence the sense of 'being done to' would be integral to the verb. The doing is inseparable from the verb as it is the essential activity. Away from the verb as central focus, nouns appear to carry out and be affected by the activity, and this is why *kartā* and *karma* are expressed separately from the verb in passive and active sentences respectively. We are so conditioned to believe that we carry out the action that we find it difficult to see the significance in Sanskrit of distinguishing between expressing the *kartā* (or *karma*) in the verb and naming it in the first noun *vibhakti*.

*Kāraka*s therefore play a fundamental part in unifying and expressing sentences. The law of three applies to them as was intimated in chapter 3.10 where they were described in three pairs. These pairs reflect basic principles of creation, cause and effect, combination and separation, and instrumentality and time/space.

Before we leave the subject of relationships within sentences, the question arises as to whether the six *kāraka*s are universal and present in every sentence. Of course, all six are rarely evident in a sentence, but are they implicit? As an example, the simple sentence 'She walked to the station' only appears to express two, *kartā* and *karma*. Yet she must have gone by some means, for some purpose, from somewhere, and at some time. All are implicit in the sentence, although not visible as not necessary to convey the meaning intended by the speaker. Take another example. 'Stop!' In Sanskrit the verb would express the *kartā* (you), but what about the other five? Something or someone is being stopped (*karma*), by some means, for some purpose, from something, and in some location. But there is no need to express them to convey the meaning of the sentence. The pervasiveness of *kārakas*, not only in sentences, but also in the formation of words (chapter 3), suggests that this may be a principle of all activity in the universe. This is explored further in the *kāraka* section of chapter 7.

5.5 Relationships in sound

The way in which the sounds of language are formed using different mouth positions and methods of articulation carries with it a diversifying tendency, distinguishing different sounds. This is, of course, essential for language, otherwise distinct words would not be formed, and meaning would not be communicated. Along with this diversifying principle, there is also a unifying principle, which operates to harmonise the juxtaposition of two or more differently formed sounds. This has already been touched on in chapter 3, but it is most evident in Sanskrit sentences, where the first or last sound of a word changes to accommodate the first or last sound of the adjacent word.

This principle operates in all languages, but explicit *sandhi* rules are not common, and appear to be much more wide-ranging in Sanskrit. In other languages they are often pronounced but not written, and hence are implicit. Here are a few implicit examples in spoken English, sometimes the result of local accent:

1. The syllable 'ed' at the end of a word is pronounced differently according to the sound preceding it. In 'walked' it becomes 't', in 'wanted' 'id', in 'rolled' 'd'.
2. The letters 't' and 'd' at the end of words may change according to the letter at the beginning of the following word. The 't' and 'y' in 'don't you' become 'ch', but 'tw' stays the same in 'don't we', and the 't' sound vanishes altogether in 'don't do'. A final 'd' and a 'y' at the beginning of the next word will normally change to 'jj' in expressions such as 'would you'. When a 't' starts the next word, the reverse process to 't' followed by 'd' occurs, so that in 'old table' the 'd' is elided.
3. One form of *sandhi* is the insertion of an additional sound to harmonise two adjoining sounds, even within the same word. For example, an additional 'p' is sometimes heard, making 'somepthing', and 'hampster'.

It may be argued that these changes in sound do not need to be recognised in formal rules or in writing because they are so slight. Yet it is clear that there are principles operating here, based on the different ways in which sounds are formed. The sounds 't' and 'd' are both dental consonants, but 't' is unvoiced and 'd' is voiced. This is rather like two notes close together on a musical scale leading to dissonance, unless this is resolved by one of the notes changing. By placing such importance on the explicit recognition of harmonious sound in speech, Sanskrit may be recognising that natural harmony which is an expression of the nature of the one Self. The sentence starts in harmony as a *sphoṭa* and ends in harmony in its full expression.

5.6 Conclusion

From these comments it is possible to see the sentence as a unity. The grammatical relationships within it form a sphere, with radii joining nouns and nominal phrases on the circumference to the verb at the centre; and the sound relationships adjust to become harmonious. This gives some indication of how the sentence also has a deeper significance. Śāntānanda Sarasvatī, in a passage about purification of the mind, speaks of the importance of understanding the proper construction of a sentence 'which is the real cosmos, which alone matters' (1973 Day 9). Seeing a sentence as 'the real cosmos' relates to the Advaitic view of creation as projection from a causal sound into multiple sounds. In *parā* there is no projection, but all is held there in potential, while in subsequent stages the sound is differentiated into many sounds until finally, it emerges as a spoken sentence at the *vaikharī* stage.

When a Sanskrit text from the Veda, the Bhagavad Gītā, or similar philosophical book, is being studied, this can involve a process of analysis and synthesis. The individual words are identified, their *dhātu*s and *pratyaya*s, and their role in the sentence, and this helps to understand the meaning of the sentence. This is an application of the classical Advaitic exercise of *vyatireka* and *anvaya*, by which the elements of the creation starting with the grossest, are identified one by one and left behind, until eventually only consciousness remains, and then each element is added back until the full creation is again present, but this time seen as an expression of consciousness, of the Self. In the context of language each word in a sentence is identified, and then the *dhātu* and *pratyaya* elements, a *vyatireka* exercise, followed by the words' role in the sentence, and the meaning of the whole sentence in context, an *anvaya* exercise. These two processes are also applied as each word is considered, which enables the full meaning of the sentence to emerge.

This brings us naturally to the subject of meaning. Without meaning the whole panoply of language, with its basic elements, its words and its sentences, would be pointless.

Chapter 6

Sound, Word and Meaning What is meaning?

6.1 What does the word 'meaning' mean?

This chapter is an exploration of the relationship between sound, word and meaning, and in particular of how to understand meaning. Meaning appears to be the most important aspect of language. After all, unless what is said conveys meaning, there is no point in saying it. It does not count as language. Is there such a thing as true meaning? In the search for truth are we not searching for meaning? Yet 'meaning' is a most elusive thing to pin down. For a start, 'meaning' (noun) and 'mean' (verb) can be understood in a variety of ways.

Consider the following sentences:

'He means to visit Edinburgh.' (intends)
'When he lifts his hand it means Yes.' (indicates)
'He means what he says.' (conveys seriousness)
'What is the meaning of life?' (purpose, point)
'What is the meaning of the word 'charity'?' (definition)
'What does Rousseau mean when he says "All men are born free"?' (conveys significance)

Not all of these uses are directly relevant to language as a conveyor of meaning, but certainly the last four are, as they are all concerned with words and sentences. The usual place to look for meaning is a dictionary, but even a small dictionary (Collins), gives nine entries for 'mean' as a verb and five for 'meaning' as a noun. Descriptions such as 'the sense or significance of a word or sentence', 'the purpose behind speech, action etc', 'the inner, symbolic or true interpretation, value or message' are most relevant to language, but like most dictionary definitions, they are little more than alternative words or phrases for the word under consideration.

What can the derivation of the word tell us, or the Sanskrit word used to denote 'meaning'? 'Meaning' comes from the Old English 'menon', which comes from the same Sanskrit source as 'mind' and 'mental', i.e. the *dhātu man* – 'to think' and also 'to understand, comprehend'. The Sanskrit word often translated as 'meaning' is *artha*. This word has a wide range of meanings in addition to 'meaning'. These include 'purpose', 'use', 'object', 'cause' and 'wealth'. The *dhātu arth*, according to Monier-Williams, means 'to point out the sense of', but in the *Dhātupāṭha* its primary sense is 'in requesting, begging, supplicating'.

It is also interesting to note that 'meaning' has the form of a present participle, as it ends with 'ing'. This gives it the quality of an activity more than an object. It is similar to words such as 'gardening', 'running' and 'opening' when used as nouns.

6.2 Levels of meaning

From this information, the diversity of which may seem bewildering, one or two features stand out. Firstly, 'meaning' is a feature of the mental or subtle realm, not the physical/material or causal/spiritual realms, although it may point to or indicate either of these other two realms. The characteristics of the mental realm are movement and fluidity.

Secondly, there can be different levels of meaning, even when considering individual words. At the first level there is the meaning of a word as a commonly accepted symbol for a physical thing such as a cup, a carpet, or a flower. However there are subtler levels of meaning, as when we speak of the concept of a table rather than a particular table, and when we move beyond physical things to words such as equality and law. At each of these levels understanding has a tendency to become fixed, which contradicts the subtle nature of meaning. One can have a fixed idea about the word 'God', 'spider', 'Jew', 'peace', or even a particular painting or table. To someone with arachnophobia, 'spider' has a meaning quite different from what is said in the dictionary. Śāntānanda Sarasvatī warned about having fixed ideas of words, saying that most of the difficulties of the world are caused by people sticking to their own set idea about a word (1971 Day 3). John Locke said much the same in the seventeenth century, as, no doubt, have many others down the ages.

Bhartṛhari speaks of levels of meaning in a different way. The first arises from abstracting a word from a sentence and analysing it grammatically. However, he sees this as a somewhat artificial activity as the subtler levels of meaning lie elsewhere. An intermediate level arises from understanding the word in the role it plays in its sentence. He regards the whole sentence as the unified speech unit (chapter 5.2), and this conveys a fuller and subtler level of meaning. The meaning of the sentence arises from the individual words, their relationships within the sentence, and the circumstances, customs and traditions within which the sentence is uttered – occasion (time and place), audience, social conventions of the time, culture etc. Take the example of ending a telephone conversation. There are conventions for doing this, which are expressed in sentences, and they act as signals to the other person that a conversation is coming to an end. It is not simply ended by one person putting the phone down, or even just saying 'Goodbye'. The sentences used may vary, but they carry an extra dimension of meaning concerned with winding down and concluding.

Dante describes four levels of meaning, which were appreciated in the mediaeval world: literal, allegorical, moral and anagogical. At the literal level words and sentences are understood at their face value; at the allegorical level they reflect a universal law or principle of nature; at the moral level they reflect a law directly related to human beings; and at the anagogical level they convey the innermost or spiritual meaning.

There is another way of seeing levels of meaning in language. Śāntānanda Sarasvatī spoke of Sanskrit words having meanings at three levels, material, mental and spiritual, and gave the example of the compound word *suddhyupāsya*, which can mean ' elder in a village' (material), 'teacher' (mental), and 'God' (spiritual).

Levels of Meaning

Increasing subtlety → →

1. A particular thing eg this table	General concept of something eg table	Abstract concept of something eg peace	
2. Word analysis	Role of word in sentence	Sentence	Sentence in context
3. Literal	Allegorical	Moral	Anagogical
4. Material	Mental	Spiritual/causal	

When these various ways of understanding levels of meaning are brought together, a trend becomes apparent. Meanings can be very limited, as when a particular physical object is being identified – apple, jam-jar, snake. They can take on a subtler sense when a word is used, for example, as an analogy, such as when someone is referred to as a snake or 'the apple of my eye.' They can be wider in scope, as when they combine into a simple sentence such as – 'Would you like to continue reading this book?' and 'Do listen to what I am saying!' At a far deeper level are statements such as '*Tattvamasi*' ('That thou art') from the Chāndogya Upanishad, which have the capacity to bring out for each person new and fresh meanings and understandings each time they are studied. It is a characteristic of the finest literature that it speaks to the reader/listener at whatever level of understanding that person is capable of, and can therefore have many meanings. Passages in Shakespeare's plays have this capacity, and in a different field , so do mantras.

Nevertheless, the meaning of any statement, by its nature, must have a limit. It is the limit which gives a particular form to the meaning. As the meaning becomes subtler, so it becomes less fixed, less limited, until it reaches the limit of personal understanding, and directs the mind beyond.

6.3 What about sound?

Some of the factors contributing to meaning and some of the different types and levels of meaning have just been identified, but this information does not provide a definite answer to the question, 'Is there such a thing as true meaning, or is meaning always something which is ephemeral and changing?' This may be because no reference has yet been made to the substance which always underlies and pervades words and meanings, which is sound. Without sound there are no words and meanings.

Someone may say that, although sound underlies and pervades speech, this does not appear to be so with writing or thoughts. If someone is reading a book, or thinking, no-one else can hear what is being read or thought. However, the reader can hear what is being read, and, provided a certain level of awareness has been reached, the thinker can hear what he or she is thinking. This fact must indicate the presence of subtle sound. The difference is one of levels of manifestation, not of the presence or absence of sound. So we can proceed.

In order to examine the relationship between sounds, words and meanings from an Advaitic viewpoint, it is necessary to refer again to the Advaitic view of how the universe arises. From this view, the whole universe arises from sound, initially the one sound represented by ॐ. This sound differentiates into many sounds, which are the causes of everything in the universe. This is reflected in such statements as: 'The creation is spoken into existence', and in the first verse of the Māṇḍūkya Upanishad: 'The Word ॐ is the Imperishable; all this its manifestation. Past, present, future – everything is ॐ. Whatever transcends the three divisions of time, that too is ॐ.' And in Book VI of the Chāndogya Upanishad: 'All transformation has speech as its basis, and it is name only.' Śāntānanda Sarasvatī has said: 'The manifestation of the creation is from sound, so sounds and mantras hold the creative powers and manifest them in different forms. There is a direct connection of a mantra to a physical thing, for physical things come out of the mantras' (1973 Day 6).

This indicates that everything is composed of sound, and there is a particular sound or word which causes each entity to exist. If that sound stopped the entity would cease to exist. This is the real or natural language of the universe. The languages which human beings speak can be seen as reflections of that natural language. Indeed, mankind's creative nature is continually bringing new ideas into existence, and then naming the physical products, such as computer, aircraft, television, internet. These ideas are subtle sounds, and in order to speak about them human beings give them names. But how can these names or words reflect the natural language?

A commonly held view is that these names are just labels. These labels can come from a variety of sources: from the name of the inventor, e.g. 'hoover'; or from elements of an earlier classical language, e.g. 'telephone'; they can start life as a slang term, e.g. 'grungy'; or be appropriated from another language, e.g. 'tomato'. Words being simply labels, the link between them and their sounds and meanings is one of custom and practice. The function of sound appears to be regarded as a conveyance of words and their meanings, not a cause of them (unless one considers it as the material cause). This conveyance is limited. The words just given as examples of labelling are in English, but they may be sounded differently by different English speakers depending on which part of the world they come from. Although there have been periods in human history when great importance was placed on how words were sounded, that is not the case nowadays. In moving to other languages the variations in sound expand exponentially. There will be equivalent words meaning very much the same in many of the hundreds of other modern languages, but most of these words will be composed of quite different sound combinations compared with those contained in the English word.

From what has just been said, it appears that, certainly in modern languages, there is little causal link between sound, word and meaning, or at least such a link is not explicitly acknowledged. At the root of this view is the empirical labelling of words, and the lack of importance given to sound as anything other than a means of recognising and conveying words.

The premise that this universe arises from, and is pervaded by, sound provides a quite different view of the significance of sound in language. According to this view, sounds exist at the causal level; and words and meanings arise from them at the subtle level. Sound only exists in the present. No-one can hear a past or future sound. A recording of sounds originally made years ago is only heard in the present, so what is heard cannot be past sounds. We do of course call them sounds from the past, but this is only when the past is regarded as having as much reality as the present.

The present moment is unique. It will never appear in the same form again. Every sentence uttered or read is unique as it is heard in the present. Even if a sentence is repeated, each time the sound will be unique. Yet there is one ever-present element, without which, according to Advaita, there cannot be any sound, or indeed any present moment; and this is consciousness. This uniqueness of sound in the present moment is hardly ever acknowledged, because the mind casts a veil over the present moment and the sound in it, a veil which is made up of memories and expectations. With language, a large part of the veil is composed of fixed ideas about the meaning of words, based on past experience. The mind may only vaguely register the unique sounds arising in the present conveying the words.

6.4 Spoken sounds and the sounds of the natural language

If everything arises from sound, then maybe spoken sounds can put us in touch with the essence of things as expressed in the natural language, despite the limitation caused by labelling. But here is another problem: to put us in touch with the essence of things, speech would have to reflect cleanly and without impediment the natural language which gives rise to things. As we do not hear that natural language, how can we know whether we are reflecting it in speech? There is a further difficulty in that all languages are composed of different sounds, and different combinations of those sounds produce words. Without knowing the natural language there appears to be no way of knowing whether particular languages are better or worse at reflecting the natural language. Yet there are some helpful indicators.

The sounds of any language are contained in their alphabet, or their equivalent in those languages consisting of such elements as clicks, tones or stresses for example. The different sounds of languages were mentioned in chapters 2 and 3, and in particular the sounds of the Sanskrit language. The conclusion was that the sounds of the Sanskrit alphabet have a special order and significance, and there has been, and remains, clear and unchanging guidance on methods of articulation and precisely where to produce the sounds in the vocal apparatus. Considerable attention has been paid over the ages to ensure that the sounds have remained true to this guidance. Consequently, the sounding of Sanskrit texts requires a high degree of attention and a thorough knowledge of, and devotion to, the guidance. Such attention, order and devotion are indications of consciousness. Inattention, disorder and lack of devotion are indications of consciousness being obscured.

This, together with the other special qualities of the Sanskrit alphabet identified in chapter 3, suggest that it is likely to have a greater capacity than other languages to reflect the sound of the natural language. Śāntānanda Sarasvatī was very clear about this. He considered the differences between languages to be due to the quality of sound in their alphabets (1965 Day 11). As for Sanskrit he said: 'It is refined and truly natural, for it contains original laws and original sounds and their combinations' (1973 Day 7).

Yet however much we might regard these sounds of the Sanskrit alphabet as pure and reflecting the natural language, this does not enable us to say anything about linking meaning with the way sounds are combined to form words, let alone about the natural language. If such were the case it would imply that the words so formed, and the *dhātu*s and *pratyaya*s with which they are constituted, would themselves by their sound reflect the natural words which cause the natural phenomena. For example, the combination of sounds which make up *kapi* 'monkey' would reflect in some way the causal sound behind monkeys. Although there is a great deal of meaning to be uncovered about Sanskrit words by exploring their *dhātus* and *pratyayas*, this is not related to the sounds of the alphabet which make up those *dhātus*, *pratyayas*, and words. The sounds *k, a, p*, and *i*, in that order, do not reveal anything about the meaning of a monkey. In similar vein Patañjali pointed out that if sounds did directly reveal meaning, the similarity of *kupa, supa,* and *yupa* ('well', 'sauce' and 'sacrificial post' respectively) would force us either to assume that the three words and the objects denoted by them have a great deal in common, or that the letters *k, s,* and *y* express the special meanings of the objects, leaving a meaningless *upa* (Mahābhāṣya 1.32.2-10). Śāntānanda Sarasvatī confirmed this when he said: 'There are just a few sounds which would give sense of their meaning, and they are words like ॐ, Rāma and Krishna. One may pronounce them and their effect would be felt, but the same is not possible with other sounds and words. For those words one has to refer to the *dhātu* and *pratyaya* and look into the dictionary for precise meaning' (1976 Day 8). We have to conclude that there is no evidence for this kind of general link between sound, word and meaning in Sanskrit, let alone any other language.

Although words and their meanings do not themselves have this general link with sound, the sound a person makes certainly conveys their state of being, their current emotional state, their degree of presence, all of which provide essential context for the language being expressed and its meaning. The sound of a word, such as its pitch and stress, can also contribute directly to its meaning. For example, 'Yes' can be spoken in several ways, to the point of meaning its opposite. A sentence spoken in anger has a quite different meaning from one spoken in love, even though the words may be the same. The whole realm of poetry relies to a considerable extent on such features as rhythm, onomatopoeia, and alliteration. In these senses sounds contribute directly to meaning.

6.5 Sound beyond meaning

Before leaving the subject of sound, there is one more dimension of sound to examine. Various levels of meaning have already been mentioned, which are all in the subtle area. There are references by Śāntānanda Sarasvatī to sounding language in such a refined and precise way that it creates 'extra spiritual significance apart from meaning'. He considers that this is created when a Sanskrit text from the Veda (which includes the Upanishads) is recited 'in its right pitch, metre and measure with pure sounds' (1971 Day 4). This reaffirms the importance of pure pronunciation, taking the participant beyond meaning into the spiritual and causal world. It also reinforces the theme of Sanskrit being composed of pure sounds. Śāntānanda Sarasvatī goes further when he asserts: '[Sanskrit] must have all its words full of spiritual significance. In other languages, since the sounds have been distorted, the significance is lost' (1971 Day 4).

6.6 Grammar linking words and meaning

This brief investigation of some of the factors contributing to meaning, and identification of the limits of sound's contribution to words and meaning, leads naturally to the subject of links just between words and meaning. This concerns the links between the grammatical principles governing the formation of words and sentences, and their meaning. These grammatical principles formed much of the content of chapters 4 and 5, and were seen as forming the bedrock of language, and in particular its structure. An analogy with the human body may help here. Without the skeleton of grammatical structure and the flesh of words and sentences, the activity of meaning will not happen. Extending the analogy further, sound can be seen as the life-force, as air/breath is the basis of the sounds of language. The table summarises this view.

Human Body	**Language**
Life-force	Sound
Skeleton	Grammar
Flesh and blood	Words and sentences
Activities	Meanings

Activities arise from the coherent functioning of the whole body, and similarly meaning arises from the coherence of sound, grammar and words in sentences.

As grammatical principles have already been considered in earlier chapters, it is only necessary here to list the main grammatical concepts which enable linkages to be made between words and meanings. Grammar differentiates words into their distinct roles as verbs, nouns, adjectives, pronouns, particles etc; verbs into conveying time, mood, person and number concerning action; nouns and pronouns into conveying number, gender and relationship of entities to the action; and particles and conjunctions into unifying the parts of a sentence. These are all essential to the conveyance of meaning.

A simple example of the importance of grammar in conveying meaning is in the title of the recent book on punctuation, 'Eats Shoots and Leaves'. Although the point of the title was to show the importance of the comma, it also shows how treating 'shoots' and 'leaves' as verbs instead of nouns dramatically changes the meaning.

In Sanskrit there are further levels of grammar describing how words themselves are formed using *dhātu*s and *pratyaya*s. *Kāraka* principles, which are so clearly and precisely expressed through Sanskrit grammar, including most of the *pratyaya*s, add a whole level of meaning to the language. The richness of grammar apparent in Sanskrit words and sentences conveys much greater subtleties and depths of meaning than other languages, which do not explicitly have such depth of grammar. Hence there is much value in analysing words in a Sanskrit sentence to identify their *dhātus* and *pratyaya*s, and which *kāraka*s apply. It would be a mistake, however, to think that the meaning of a word lies in its analysis. That is only part of the story. Indeed Socrates warns in 'Cratylus' (436): 'He who follows names in the search after things, and analyses their meaning, is in great danger of being deceived.' He justifies this view by arguing that the person who first gave a name to something may have been mistaken in his conception of that thing.

6.7 Meaning and activity

Having considered the contributions to meaning available from dictionary definitions, from different levels of meaning, sound and grammatical analysis, we can now turn to the contribution to meaning afforded by activity, function and use. This has been mentioned in passing several times in this chapter, starting with the fact that the word 'meaning' itself is in the form of a present participle, ending in 'ing.'

Meaning is commonly associated with things, but it is really concerned with activity. Śāntānanda Sarasvatī has said that words mean what they do. The full quotation is '*Brahman* or *Ātman* has the mantra or the word, and these words become forms, for they each mean what the word says and they do what the word implies' (1978 Day 5). He gave as an example the word 'fire', which can be used with many meanings. Its meaning depends on its use or function. Wittgenstein came to a similar conclusion that the meaning of a word is in its use. As an example, he gave the instance of pointing to a piece on a chess board and saying: 'This is a king'. To someone who knows how to play chess, meaning here will lie in the use of that particular piece in the game, its role and function. This can apply to any sentence. Furthermore, the meaning intended by the speaker can only be fully understood when there is appreciation of the word, grammatically as well as empirically; of the grammatical structure of the statement containing the word; and of the situation and circumstances in which the statement is made, including the state of the person speaking. Another example may help. The word 'Tigers' emitted during a discussion about species in danger of extinction will have a quite different meaning from the same word uttered while in a jeep in a safari park.

Śāntānanda Sarasvatī is even more radical than this. He equates meaning with experience. Words in themselves are 'innocent' unless they are identified with. So, pain is simply a word to someone witnessing another in pain, but to the person who has the pain and therefore experiences and identifies with it, the word 'pain' has real meaning at that time (1987 Day 3). The word 'pain' will give knowledge to the doctor, but meaning to the person experiencing it.

6.8 Conclusions on meaning

It is now possible to bring together the various factors which contribute to meaning, and draw some conclusions.

- Sounds and their combinations provide the substance of language, which is then shaped by grammar to form words and meanings in sentences. Sounds can contribute to meaning but do not in themselves usually form complete meanings in language.
- The laws of grammar are fundamental in forming words, sentences and their meanings. Languages differ in the depth and comprehensiveness of their grammars.
- Words have meaning, but there is great danger in believing the meaning is fixed.

- Meaning can be investigated by analysing the grammar of a sentence or statement and also the grammar and etymology of individual words through their *dhātu*s and *pratyaya*s, and the findings can make significant contributions to meaning.
- Circumstance, custom and practice usually play a large part in determining meaning. This includes some or all of: the time and place; audience; social conventions; culture; assumptions held in common; the relationship between the people concerned etc.
- Meaning is intimately connected with the use and function of words, with what they do, with whether what is signified by words is being experienced and identified with at that moment.
- Meaning is a creature of the subtle or mental world, and therefore has a fluid, unfixed quality.
- Meanings have limits, although those limits can vary enormously. As a corollary, the same word or expression can have meanings at many different levels: physical, mental, emotional and spiritual, for example.

From this it is clear that meanings are very much concerned with the ever-changing nature of creation. The meaning is in the moment. In the next moment the meaning changes, because the factors contributing to the meaning have changed, even if the same sentence is heard or read. Failures in communication of meaning occur when the speaker and hearer have different fixed ideas about the meaning of the words being uttered, when the words are being heard through a particular emotional state, or some of the factors contributing to meaning are not evident. How often have we heard a wise statement and said 'I have heard that many times, but never appreciated that it meant this.'

Bhartṛhari calls appreciation of meaning a *pratibhā*, usually translated as a flash of insight or intuition. At that point, the *sphoṭa* of the speaker or writer has been expressed in sentences, which have been received and understood by the hearer. The circle is complete.

Meaning is a feature of creation, of *Māyā*, of that which has been called illusion. If, by 'true', we mean what is concerned with the unchanging, eternal reality, then we cannot speak of a true meaning, as meaning is concerned with the changing, unreal illusion. It would be better to speak of a correct appreciation of the meaning, that is, what the speaker or writer intended to convey.

This conclusion has significant implications for our attitude to meaning, and how we appreciate it. As meaning is understood in the present moment, it is not something which lasts, although its effects may well last, even for a lifetime. Trying to hold on to meaning is trying to fix it. Meaning by nature is fluid, and fixing it turns it into something else, having more of the quality of the material world. Water is by nature fluid. When frozen it is no longer water. We call it ice. The same happens with meaning. When frozen it is no longer meaning. We may call it memory. More often we make no distinction between meaning in the moment and fixed meaning. When we are experiencing the world through a veil of fixed meanings, it may seem ordinary and flat, or highly charged and evocative. When we do not hang on to meanings, they are fresh and immediate. The world really is meaningful in the present.

1 *The Dialogues of Plato* trans B. Jowett, Random House

Chapter 7

Pāṇinian grammar: some special features

7.1 In considering how far Sanskrit reflects Advaitic principles, I have made several references to the famous Sanskrit grammar, Pāṇini's *Aṣṭādhyāyī*. Although this work is essentially a descriptive grammar, which does not consider the principles of the language or the reasons for its grammatical laws, Advaitic principles are clearly evident. This chapter describes some aspects of the *Aṣṭādhyāyī* which provide evidence of this.

The *Aṣṭādhyāyī*

The *Aṣṭādhyāyī*, literally 'That which has eight Chapters', consists of just under 4000 sutras, which describe the grammatical laws for the formation of Sanskrit words, and their combination in compound words and in sentences. It was composed some 2,500 years ago, and has been regarded ever since as the most complete, succinct and authoritative grammar of Sanskrit ever written, and, some would say, of any language. Leonard Bloomfield, the American who developed structural linguistics in the first half of the twentieth century, called it 'one of the greatest monuments of human intelligence' (Language 1933). Noam Chomsky has also acknowledged his debt to Pāṇini in developing his concepts of generative and deep grammar.

Questions of Sanskrit grammar have been, and continue to be, referred back to the *Aṣṭādhyāyī* for resolution. The *Aṣṭādhyāyī* was composed at the end of a long line of Sanskrit grammars, and is regarded as the culmination of those works. Because the work is written in sutras, many of the laws are extremely cryptic, requiring explanation for most readers. A sutra may simply say 'not at the end of a *pada* (word)' or 'the letter *o*', because the remaining words in the sutra are understood from earlier sutras in a particular sequence of related sutras.

There are six types of sutra. The principal one, called *vidhi*, states a grammatical law, such as: 'In place of a *m* at the end of a word before a word beginning with a consonant, there is an *anusvāra* (a nasal sound expressed only through the nose)'. A *sañjñā* sutra defines a grammatical term used in the *Aṣṭādhyāyī*, such as : 'V*riddhi* when it appears in a sutra means a long *ā*, *ai* and *au*' – this is the very first sutra in the *Aṣṭādhyāyī*. A *paribhāṣā* sutra is explanatory, helping with the interpretation of *vidhi* sutras, such as: 'When the sixth case is used for a word in a sutra it has the sense "in the place of "'. An *adhikāra* sutra governs a number of sutras which follow it. It can be like a chapter heading, or it can be a rule which applies to a group of following sutras. At the beginning of the third chapter of the *Aṣṭādhyāyī* there is a sutra which simply says *Pratyayaḥ*. This means that all the sutras in this chapter and also the fourth and fifth chapters are about *pratyaya*s. The remaining two types of sutra are called *niyama*, which restricts the scope of a *vidhi* sutra, and *pratiṣedha,* which prohibits it. An example is the sutra 'Not at the end of a word' which limits the scope of a preceding sutra specifying when a dental *n* changes to a cerebral *ṇ*.

7.2 *It* letters

A striking feature of Pāṇini's grammar is the widespread use of indicatory letters, called *it* letters, in his sutras. They form a metalanguage, containing information about the language element to which they are attached, elements such as *dhātu*s, *pratyaya*s, single letters and groups of letters in the *Māheśvara* sutras. For example an *it t* added after an *a* indicates that only a short *a* is meant, whereas when an *it l* is added after an *a* this signifies the whole of the Sanskrit alphabet. There are several hundred of these *it* expressions which mean different things according to whether they come at the beginning or end of a grammatical element, and to which element they are joined. They are not seen outside the context of grammar, and more particularly outside of a Pāṇinian sutra, and are used solely to help describe how the rules work. In recent times they have been acknowledged as the forerunner to the standard method of design for computer languages.

Because they convey packets of grammatical information in only one or two letters, they considerably reduce the number of words needed to explain Sanskrit grammar. This concentrates the mind when digesting or remembering grammatical laws, as a minimum amount of sound is needed. To speak about the alphabet, all that is needed is *al,* and to speak about the voiced consonants and semi-vowels together, the single syllable *haś* is sufficient. More complex information is also conveyed by *it* letters. The *it* letters *ślu* tell us that when the third class of *dhātu*s is conjugated, the first syllable of the *dhātu* is reduplicated in certain tenses and moods.

7.3 Different types of invisibility

It letters are invisible outside the context of grammatical rules. Pāṇini makes quite clear that there is a difference between removal and invisibility. Although these letters are invisible, their effects continue to apply. This is so even if the grammatical element to which they were attached undergoes several more grammatical operations before reaching its final form. To make clear the difference between invisibility and removal Pāṇ ini states that *it* letters are replaced by something called *lopa,* which means 'invisible yet still operative'. This may appear an unnecessary subtlety, until one hears that there are several levels of invisibility! It is important in Sanskrit grammar to know which type of invisibility is being spoken about. It is not enough just to say that something becomes invisible. That is too vague. Characteristics of this grammar are brevity, precision and clarity, and this is very evident here.

The closer something is to its source and the further from its final expression in the universe, the less visible, and more subtle and powerful it is. These are the characteristics of *it* letters. The source of everything is the Absolute, the Word. The Upanishads speak of this source as 'the most subtle'. In this context 'subtle' carries the sense of something which is minute when viewed from the level of full expression, yet very powerful as it contains the power which shapes the full expression. Atoms are minute, yet contain enormous energy, which has vast effects when released. *It* letters are rather like atoms or a molecule of DNA, as through their specific activities they channel the release of energy to shape words.

Concepts of invisibility apply not just to *it* letters, but to other expressions or elements of language in a sutra. Some *pratyaya*s disappear after they have joined with a *dhātu*, and are only known because of the effects they leave behind. For example, a *kvip pratyaya* joins with a *dhātu* to form a *prātipadika* or word stem. It then disappears, but its effect on the *dhātu* remains, having changed it into a word stem. This concept of invisibility is called *lopa*, which means that whatever is replaced by *lopa* continues to have the same effect as though it were still there. Another type of invisibility, called *luk*, means the opposite, that is, whatever it replaces no longer continues to have any effect on subsequent grammatical operations. It is as though it does not exist. In between *lopa* and *luk* come two other types of invisibility, *ślu* and *lup*. Although *ślu* causes that which it has replaced to have no further effect on subsequent grammatical operations, it also causes the *dhātu* to which it is 'joined' to reduplicate. The other term, *lup*, is selective in preventing effects, in that, unlike *luk*, it retains the gender and number of the original word in the derivative word.

There is a yet further type of invisibility in the *Aṣṭādhyāyī*. An example of this is the sutra *pūrvatrāsiddham* which can be translated as 'Sutras preceding this sutra in the *Aṣṭādhyāyī* treat sutras subsequent [to *pūrvatrāsiddham*] as though they have not taken effect.' In other words, preceding sutras do not see the operation of subsequent sutras. This sutra comes at the beginning of the second chapter of the eighth and final book of the *Aṣṭādhyāyī* and governs the subsequent 300 or so sutras. When any sutra in this section operates, its effect is invisible to any preceding sutra in the *Aṣṭādhyāyī*. This is particularly important when laws expressed by *sandhi* sutras could apply. These sutras appear both before and after *pūrvatrāsiddham*, but those before it cannot change a form produced by a sutra after it. This is not easy to explain to anyone who has not studied *sandhi*, but I will attempt to do so with an example. When *Hare* is before *iti* it becomes *Haray*. *Haray iti* then becomes *Hara iti* due to a sutra which comes after *pūrvatrāsiddham*. A sutra which comes before *pūrvatrāsiddham* states that *a*+*i* becomes *e*, so one might expect *Hara iti* to become *Hareti*. However, this sutra is made ineffective by *pūrvatrāsiddham*; thus *Hara iti* is the final form. In this way, whole swathes of grammatical law are made inoperative in particular circumstances and appear to be invisible.

The importance of invisibility in Sanskrit grammar reflects the importance of invisibility in the laws of the universe. The most significant forces which shape our world are invisible: electromagnetism; gravity; light (what we see are reflections of light, not light itself); space; air. These are very different types of invisibility, just as there are different types identified by Pāṇini.

7.4 The *kāraka* sutras, and their deeper significance

The *kāraka*s can be seen as expressing universal laws through the medium of language. When so recognised they enable us to see beyond the surface appearance to deeper levels of things and activities. All actions in the mental and material realms have certain common characteristics, which are always present, whether expressed or not. The same applies to sentences. Every action takes place somewhere, and every sentence is stating something which has a location; every action has a cause and an effect, and every sentence contains a cause and an effect, even if it is merely implicit. Every action comes from somewhere and is going somewhere, and every sentence also contains these two directions, sometimes explicitly, sometimes implicitly.

We will recall that the six *kāraka*s are called *kartā, karma, karaṇam, sampradānam, apādānam*, and *adhikaraṇam* (chapter 3.9). For each *kāraka* Pāṇini gives a sutra which explains its essential meaning. These sutras can be understood at several different levels. At the grammatical level they are describing the role of a word in a sentence; at the mental level, the role or state of a person or thing; and at the causal or spiritual level they are describing the Absolute or the Self. An exposition of these sutras follows.

The first sutra consists of only one word: *kārake*. This translates as 'in relation to the action' and Pāṇini intends this phrase to be read into the following sutras which are all about *kāraka* starting with *kartā*.

Kartā

Sutra *Svatantraḥ kartā (kārake)*

Svatantra that which has the system within itself; that which is self-dependent

That which has the system for the action within itself is called the *kartā*, the agent

The system within may be of greater or lesser scope. In the grammar of a sentence the *kartā* is the independent agent, the principal actor for organising and carrying out the activity described in the sentence. The speaker or writer chooses who or what is the *kartā*. In life individuals may be *kartā* in a particular area. One is a carpenter, another an engineer and so on. These individuals will be using the skills of carpentry or engineering. The usefulness of anyone depends upon the system which they have within themselves. This system may be very limited, related just to their own benefit, or wider, so that the needs of the community, the nation, or the whole of humanity are encompassed in the activity performed by the *kartā*. At the causal or spiritual level the *kartā* is the initiator. In Advaita, for this creation to come about, there must be a *kartā*, having the system of the entire cycle of creation within itself. That is the Creator or creative force.

Karma

Sutra *Karturīpsitatamam karma (kārake)*

kartur of the agent

īpsitatamam that which is most wanted

That which is most wanted by the *kartā* in relation to the action is called *karma*.

In relation to an action *karma* is the object. In a grammatical context 'most wanted' has the sense of 'most directly connected with the *kartā*,', or 'most immediately aimed at by the *kartā*'. There is a companion sutra which extends the meaning to include 'not most wanted' i.e. dislike or indifference. At the mental level, *karma* can mean action, result or fate, which lead to other interesting interpretations of this sutra. At the spiritual level, that which is really wanted is the Self. Whatever the multitude of changing personal desires, that which is most wanted, that which underlies them all, is the Self, because its nature is truth, consciousness, and bliss, *sat*, *cit,* and *ānanda.*

Karaṇam

Sutra *Sādhakatamam karaṇam (kārake)*

Sādhakatamam that which is most effective

That which is most effective for the accomplishment of an action is called *karaṇa.*

In relation to an action, *karaṇa* is the instrument, the means by which it is accomplished. In English sentences the words 'by', 'with' and 'through' can indicate this. That which is most effective for completing the job in hand may be a brush, a screwdriver or an aircraft at the physical level. At the mental level, it may be the right words, the right emotion, the right role. These can all be *karaṇa*. The most effective instrument at the spiritual level can be seen as the presence of the Self, with its limitless consciousness, knowledge, and bliss.

Sampradānam

Sutra *Karmaṇā yamabhipraiti sa sampradānam (kārake)*

karmaṇā connected with the action

yam to whom or to which

abhipraiti one intends or is devoted to

sa sampradānam that (*sa*) is called *sampradānam*

That to which one intends to connect the action is called *sampradānam*

In English grammar this is called the indirect object, and in Latin the dative: that to which something is given. 'He gives her a gift': 'her' is dative. In the mental area, whatever one performs is devoted to or intended for something, some power, good or bad, useful or harmful. An action is always dedicated to something, as there will always be an intention in mind, for the action to be performed. Ultimately, everything is dedicated only to the Self which pervades everything, and in its spiritual sense *sampradānam* therefore stands for the Self.

Apādānam

Sutra	*Dhruvamapāye'pādānam (kārake)*
Dhruvam	the unmoving
apāye	in moving away from
apādānam	is called *apādānam*

In relation to an action the unmoving from which movement comes is called *apādānam*.

At the level of an action, there will always be something which is unmoving relative to it. In the sentence 'He fell from the car', 'from the car' is *apādānam*, even though the car may be travelling very fast. 'Car' is the unmoving element in relation to the action of falling. The following sentences offer examples from the mental world: 'From attachment arises desire'; 'He spoke from experience'. At the causal level *apādānam* can be seen as another name for the Self. *Dhruvam* means eternal as well as unmoving, and that which is ever unmoving can only be the Self; everything in creation is moving.

Adhikaraṇam

Sutra	*Ādhāro'dhikaraṇam (kārake)*
Ādhāraḥ	substratum
ādhikaraṇam	is called *adhikaraṇam*

In relation to an action the substratum is called *adhikaraṇam*

This *kāraka* concerns the location of an action, where or when it is taking place. In an English sentence 'in' or 'on' indicate its presence, as in ' in the wood' and 'on Wednesday'. Hence, in grammar, it is the locative case. Actions take place in a mental or emotional state, which can be seen as the expression of this *kāraka* at that level. Actions are undertaken in love, in anger, in states of confusion, dreaminess, tiredness. Ultimately the substratum of mental and physical locations is that which underlies everything. In Advaita, that is the substance of the Absolute, which is pure consciousness. *Adhikaraṇam* is eternally present, all-pervading, and one. All action takes place in the substance of the Absolute, the realm of consciousness. The sutra can therefore be interpreted as 'The substance of the Absolute is *adhikaraṇam*, the place and time in which every action is performed'.

These six sutras can be understood as showing these six *kāraka*s, six forms of expression, at all levels of creation, causal, mental and material, and as reflected in language, and explicitly in the Sanskrit language. These forms of expression can be seen as cause and effect (*kartā* and *karma*), fusion and fission (*sampradānam* and *apādānam*), and instrument and supreme instrument (*karaṇam* and *adhikaraṇam*).

7.5 Beyond *kāraka*, beyond relationship

Kāraka, as the word indicates, is concerned with relationship to the activity. The activity itself is expressed by the *kriyā* or verb. However we have seen that the relationship of *kartā* or *karma* is still expressed in the verbal suffix, producing active and passive voices. Pāṇini also describes an impersonal usage called *bhāva,* which is not directly available in English. Here the verbal suffix can express the activity itself, with no active or passive relationship. As an example take *gamyate,* the nearest English to which would be 'it is gone' where 'it' is impersonal, not signifying anything in particular. The sentence might be *mayā gamyate* 'it is gone by me' or, as we would say, 'I go'. The subtle difference here is that the speaker is emphasising the activity of going, not who goes. Pāṇini also describes how a *bhāva* sense can be carried by a non-verbal suffix to show completed activity. It shows itself in words such as *tyāga* (renunciation), *pāka* (cooking), and *rāga* (colouring), derived from the *dhātu*s *tyaj, pac,* and *rañj* respectively, with the addition of a suffix. Here the noun is simply expressing the completed state of the activity of the *dhātu*. The activity of renouncing leads to renunciation, the activity of cooking leads to the state of cooking, and the activity of colouring leads to the state of colouring. There is no *kartā* or *karma* in the word. *Bhāva* is also used more generally in Sanskrit to describe the sense of the *dhātu*. A *dhātu* is not a word, so a word has to be used in order to give some sense of it. For example, the *bhāva* sense of the *dhātu bhū* is *sattāyām*, meaning 'in pure existence'.

It may appear that *bhāva* is expressing no more than subtle gradations of meaning, but its deeper significance lies in showing the essence of the creative process. Stages of creation were summarised in chapter 4.8, but here more is revealed, firstly in the form of the impersonal verb, which appears between the *dhātu* stage and the active or passive verbal stage, and secondly in nouns which only express completed activity without any *kāraka*.

Both point to the Self as neither the one who hears, sees, touches etc, *kartā,* nor what is heard, seen or touched, *karma,* but as the hearing, seeing, touching itself. That is where consciousness is.

7.6 'I' and 'You'

There is a very interesting affinity between the *sarvanāmas* 'I' and 'You' in the grammatical laws expressed in the Pāṇini sutras which describe their development. Although the final forms themselves are very varied, and far removed from their stem forms *asmad,* 'I', and *yuṣmad,* 'You', each of the twenty one sutras which describe how these forms develop, applies to both pronouns. As an example one sutra says 'When *ṅas* (the affix for the sixth case singular) follows, *tava* and *mama* are the substitutes of *yuṣmad* and *asmad* respectively.' There is also a very close affinity between the sound of the two words in their stem form. The only difference is in their initial syllables, *a* for 'I' and *yu* for 'You' (the cerebral *ṣ* in *yuṣmad* replaces the dental *s* because the preceding vowel is *u*).

Thus, at the levels of both sound and law, these two words are very close. This can be seen as a reflection of the close similarity at the spiritual level between 'I' and 'You'. Essentially I am you, the differences lying in the mental and material worlds, not the causal world.

While on the subject of 'I' and 'You', it is interesting to note that many forms of these Sanskrit words are echoed in many modern European languages. All singular forms of *asmad* begin with *m* except for the nominative *aham.* This is reflected in the singular forms such as *mama* 'my', 'ma', 'mein', 'mio'. The nominative forms do vary but some affinity with *aham* can still be seen: 'I', 'ich', 'je', 'io'. The plural forms have the sound *va* in the nominative and *asm* in all other forms. So *vayam* is reflected in 'we', 'wir', and *asmān* in 'us', 'uns' but not in the French 'nous' or Italian 'noi'. The singular forms of *yuṣmad* all begin with the letter *t* and the plurals with *yu*; so, for example, *tvam* and *yuvan* are reflected in 'thou' and 'you', 'tu' and 'vous', 'tu' and 'voi', 'du' and 'ihr'.

7.7 From unity to diversity

Initially the law is one, according to Advaita, and only as creation lawfully unfolds does it become increasingly visible and apparently complex. This process can be described as coming into manifestation, or as moving from unity to diversity. Pāṇini demonstrates this in a number of ways, but one substantial example will suffice here.

In speaking about tenses and moods, and the verbal endings which express them, Pāṇini starts with one syllable, *la*. The *a* is for pronunciation, so we are just left with *l*. This letter is the starting point for all the tenses, moods and conjugational suffixes (*pratyayas*). They are all contained in this one letter. The first move outwards is made with the names for the ten tenses and moods, which all begin with this letter *l*. The present tense is called *laṭ*, the imperative *loṭ*, one of the three past tenses *laṅ*, and so on. The next step takes place when eighteen conjugational suffixes replace *l* and the tenses and moods it represents. There are two sets of nine suffixes, each portraying singular, dual and plural for the three persons, called first, second, and third in English grammar. The essential reason, although not the only one, for there being two sets is that one expresses the active voice and the other the passive voice. This is not the end of the process of differentiation, as each of these eighteen suffixes may be substituted by other forms in particular situations, such as a particular tense or mood, or when the stem of the verb ends in a particular letter. Expressing this in tabular form shows more clearly the growth in diversity and complexity.

la	One sound containing all that follows
laṭ liṭ luṭ lṛt leṭ loṭ laṅ liṅ luṅ lṛṅ	Ten tenses and moods (called *lakāras*)

tip tas jhi sip thas tha mip vas mas ta ātām jha thās āthām dhvam iṭ vahi mahiṅ	A set of 18 conjugational suffixes (nine expressing the active voice and nine the passive) applied to each of the ten *lakāras*, making 180 forms
Substitutes for the 180 suffixes	These substitute suffixes relate to particular situations, such as one of the *lakāras*, or a particular *dhātu* or group of *dhātus*, and lead to hundreds more forms

This is a reflection of the creative process, both in the mental and the physical world. In nature a tree begins with a seed, which develops into a seedling with one or two leaves, a sapling with one main branch, twigs and leaves, a young tree with several branches, many twigs and leaves, and finally a fully grown tree with many branches, producing many seeds and many more trees. In human life, someone has an idea for harnessing the powers of nature to fulfil a human desire. It is developed by experimentation, and then by speaking and writing about it. Physical objects are produced, and if the invention or creation is useful or enjoyable, in due course many more are produced. Ideas sprout, are developed by argument and dissertation, and some come to rule over a nation or a culture. Whole civilisations grow from the words and acts of a great teacher.

7.8 Conclusions

Pāṇini's great work is acknowledged by linguists across the centuries and civilisations, and by some from other disciplines such as cybernetics and mathematics. It is, by any valuation, an extraordinary feat of composition. Yet that in itself does not provide evidence of holding within it the principles of Advaita or, to put it another way, of showing that Sanskrit is a clear reflection of the natural language. For that we have to look beyond the complexity and subtlety of the work to identify some principles which have an affinity with Advaita.

I suggest that there is some evidence for this in the topics touched on in this chapter:

- the *it* letters with their characteristics of invisibility, subtlety and shaping power;
- the significance of invisibility in the grammar, reflecting its significance in creation;
- the *kārakas* expressing six fundamental relationships in activity, which apply throughout the development of words and sentences;
- *bhāva* which is concerned with pure activity (oneness), without any relationship (duality);
- the affinity between 'I' and 'You' in Sanskrit grammar and sound, reflecting the essential unity of these two 'names of all' or *sarvanāma*s;
- how Pāṇini describes the development of Sanskrit words using the principle of a simple unit expressing itself through diversity.

All of these examples can be seen as reflecting the natural process of creation.

Chapter 8

Laws of Sanskrit reflecting natural laws?

8.1 There have been several threads running through this book: the nature of human language; its relation to the natural laws of the universe; the basic elements of language and how they come together to form meaningful speech. These threads are united by a common theme, the relation of language to truth. Such a general theme has been given focus by considering the Advaitic view of truth and by concentrating on the Sanskrit language, although by no means exclusively. I hope that by this stage it will be apparent that there is much in Sanskrit which expresses Advaitic principles. What remains is to draw these threads together.

Although much has been said in previous chapters about links between Advaitic principles and Sanskrit, this has only occasionally addressed the question of links between laws of language and laws of science. When laws of physics are considered, they seem very differently expressed from chemical or biological laws, let alone laws of language. A grammatical sutra appears to have little in common with a law of thermodynamics, or the law describing how the area of a right-angled triangle is calculated. The nature of these fields is different, and the laws are expressed in quite different terms. However, if the question is rephrased to speak of principles rather than laws, this opens up a more fruitful line of enquiry. The principles which began to be examined explicitly in chapter 2, and then implicitly in subsequent chapters, were unity, sound, lawfulness, consciousness, reflectivity and stability. Examination of them can provide indications of commonality in these apparently different fields.

8.2 Unity in diversity

The first principle examined was the unity pervading movement from unmanifest singularity to manifest diversity. In Sanskrit grammar we have seen this, for instance, in the development from a *dhātu* to a fully inflected word, from the single syllable *la* to the multifarious verbal inflections; in the pervasive nature of the sound *a*; and in languages generally with the expansion from *sphoṭa* to sentence. In biology it can be seen in the development from a single seed to a fully formed living entity, from the genetic code in DNA to a human being, from stem cells to a particular part of the body. Similarly, starting in quantum physics with an abstract unitary object or vibration, a quark, there is an expansion into what is experienced and evident in the sensory world. In human society the principle can be seen in the teaching or thought of men as diverse in their message as Christ and Marx, where whole societies have been shaped by their teaching or political philosophy.

Another aspect of the principle of unity is expressed in the natural tendency to bond or harmonise. In Sanskrit more than in any other language this is expressed in the laws of *sandhi*, which operate both within and between words, to provide harmonious sound. In chemistry, this is seen in the combination of chemicals to form new substances; in biology, where male and female unite to produce offspring; in law, where the issue between two parties is resolved by the judge and jury, and between nations when a treaty is agreed. In fact, at any interface of two differing substances, qualities, or people there is a reaction, and changes occur to produce a new situation. The two entities can be physical, biological, musical, cultural, psychological, grammatical or mathematical, to name but a few. Unless some accommodation, combination or *sandhi* takes place between the entities concerned, their separateness remains dominant, with effects such as war between nations, musical dissonance, an interval between words, over-specialisation of species, ghettos, and Acts of Parliament which are unworkable or have unintended effects. Appendix 2 has more to say on this subject.

8.3 Stability and Lawfulness

Sandhi is also a major force in maintaining the stability of Sanskrit. In language, as in other spheres, there are inherent tendencies for change which will take place unless there are countervailing influences. These changes are due to natural features such as the structure of the mouth, and the consequent ease or difficulty in pronouncing certain sounds when they are juxtaposed. In Sanskrit these forces for natural change are accommodated and regulated without affecting the stability of the language. By explicitly recognising natural tendencies to change, such as a final *m* in a word changing to the nasal consonant with the same mouth position as that of the consonant starting the next word, the integrity of the original form and sound of the word is maintained, with temporary changes being regulated and harmonised when such situations arise. In this way consistency is always maintained between the sound and the written form of the language. Without this principle so strongly uniting sound and form, languages inevitably diverge in their written and spoken forms. The more this connection is lost, the less transparency, simplicity, lawfulness and stability there is in the language.

Sandhi laws are only one element of the grammatical laws of Sanskrit. Most grammatical laws are concerned directly with the formation of words, setting out each step explicitly, so there is no doubt how the final form arises. If language is to reflect the principles governing the natural world, it must be entirely lawful, because that is how all natural processes and entities operate. If the laws of language are not explicit, the language will develop arbitrary and inconsistent forms, leading to a lack of clarity and eventually to different languages, as has happened throughout human history.

Stability is of course a feature of law generally. Laws of physics, mechanics or mathematics do not change, even though their expression may differ greatly with differing situations, and the way of describing them may change with greater understanding. In this respect Sanskrit with its unchanging grammatical laws mirrors natural laws.

8.4 Sound

Sounds which are heard in human language come within a certain range of vibrations or energy waves. We also experience or register other types of vibrations, such as light waves producing colour, ultra-violet and infra-red vibrations, electro-magnetic waves, X-rays and radiation. All matter has been described as vibrating energy, and would not exist without vibration. This principle of vibration appears to be basic to this universe.

The sound vibrations which form human language are extremely subtle. The capacity of the human mind to be aware of these subtleties is amazing. In recent years scientists have developed equipment which can monitor a baby's awareness of phonetic sounds at birth, and have identified that this awareness extends to over 600 such sounds. Yet within the first year of life the awareness has diminished to only 40 to 50 sounds, those used in the local language. All the other phonetic sounds are still heard, but are not registered as conscious experiences. The particular sounds which are still registered will therefore carry special importance in the life of the individual.

For humans some vibrations are beneficial, while others are lethal. In the spectrum of sounds which give rise to human language it would therefore be reasonable to assume that some are more beneficial than others. This is where the Sanskrit language is unique among languages. The basic sounds are structured in such a way that they produce harmonious resonances when correctly sounded. This is supported by the views of those who have become proficient in producing these sounds. For example Śāntānanda Sarasvatī has said: 'Sanskrit is refined and truly natural for it contains original laws and original sounds and their combinations' (Day 7 1973). Dr Vyaas Houston, the American yoga and Sanskrit teacher, said in a conversation about Sanskrit in 1992: 'The Sanskrit alphabet is a coherent selection of the most pure, distinct and focussed sounds that can be made by the human vocal instrument.' He has likened learning to sound Sanskrit to learning to play a musical instrument, where you tune in to the basic mouth positions and appreciate the sensitivities of each vibration. The special nature of the Sanskrit alphabet was considered in chapter 3.

8.5 Reflectivity and Consciousness

These two principles are interrelated, as the former mirrors the latter. Without reflectivity there would be no way of recognising consciousness. We say that inanimate objects have no consciousness. It would be more accurate to say that inanimate objects do not exhibit conscious features, such as life and the capacity to reproduce, responsiveness to sensory impressions, emotion, and especially the ability to speak. These features reflect consciousness, rather as light itself is not seen, but only reflections of aspects of it in the colour spectrum. If light enters or passes through anything without any of it being reflected, it is invisible, as in space or blackness. Similarly, consciousness is not evident if it is not reflected.

Human language has the extraordinary capacity to reflect all three worlds, material, mental and spiritual, and has been identified as that characteristic which distinguishes humanity from all other species. How accurately and fully it reflects these worlds is a measure of its level of consciousness. The difference between languages in this respect was discussed in chapter 2.8, and evidence for Sanskrit being the most conscious language has been put forward in subsequent chapters.

The most reflective substance is that which by its very nature is reflective, is very finely constructed and polished, has no imperfections in its structure, and is facing or angled towards the subject of reflection. Then it will be able to reflect the subject accurately. Language is by its nature reflective, as explained in this extract from the quotation in chapter 4.1 from Bhartṛhari: 'Here (in the science of grammar) the word is of two kinds. It is eternal and it is a product. The product is that which is found in worldly usage and it bears the reflection of the Self which is essentially the word.' At the level of science the ability of language to reflect what is would I am sure not be disputed, but there would be a difference of view in the interpretation of what is being reflected, the Self or the world, or both.

The next criterion of reflectivity is being finely constructed and polished. This is where differences between languages become evident. The purity, harmony and orderliness of the sounds used in Sanskrit have been described already, as has the lawfulness and depth of significance in the grammar forming Sanskrit words and sentences. It is hardly surprising that the very word *Saṁskṛta* means 'perfectly constructed'.

Having no imperfections in its structure may be seen as an

extension of the previous criterion, but it is worth mentioning that unless a word is constructed following Sanskrit grammatical laws, i.e. having a *dhātu* and *pratyaya*s which join together in accordance with recognised laws, it is not regarded as Sanskrit. It is also relevant to mention again the laws of *sandhi*, which, recognising certain structural features of the vocal apparatus, regulate sounds in such a way that potential imperfections and rough edges are smoothed away in the moment of enunciation.

The final criterion, facing or being angled towards that which is being reflected, may seem so obvious that it hardly needs mentioning, but in another sense it goes to the heart of what language is all about. It is self-evident that the function of language is to facilitate communication and enable the world to be described and explained as clearly and accurately as possible. But if its function is also to reflect and magnify the qualities of the Self, then this needs to be explained and demonstrated.

The fundamental nature of sound at the causal, mental and physical levels of this universe has been mentioned a number of times. As human language is a particular expression of that sound which has the inherent capacity to reflect, it would be reasonable to say that it could reflect the qualities of its source, that is, the Self.

The Self is pure existence, consciousness and bliss. A language which reflects these most is therefore the best reflector of the Self. Reflecting existence in language can be described as reflecting what is, in all three worlds, but not pure existence itself which is limitless and indescribable. Reflecting consciousness can be described as reflecting all the levels of consciousness as expressed in the universe, but not consciousness itself because that is always the subject, and not an object to be observed. Evidence for Sanskrit being the best reflector of both these qualities of the Self has been provided throughout this book.

Reflecting bliss in language can only be verified from personal experience. I can certainly support the experience of Dr Vyaas Houston when he says: '[Sanskrit's] great power lies in bringing body, mind and spirit into harmonic alignment... It facilitates an expansion of awareness, tranquillity and bliss.'

8.6 Language and truth

However fine and complete a reflector a language may be, it can never express the truth. Truth has been described at the beginning of this book in the following words: 'one, totally still, yet all-pervasive, pure, omniscient, partless, conscious and self-existent. The apparent multiplicity of the world is not real. In truth it is one.' Language is the most powerful tool used by man, but cannot by definition be equal to what has just been described. In fact, realisation of the truth involves transcending language. In the *Yoga Vāsiṣṭha* there is the statement 'As long as words are used to denote a truth, duality is inevitable: however, such duality is not the truth. All divisions are illusory.'[1] The penultimate step of the seven steps on the way of knowledge in Advaita teaching is called *padarthābhāvanī*, which translates as 'beyond word and meaning'. Nevertheless, without a language which reflects the laws of the universe the previous five steps would be far more difficult to take. This book has explored some of the features of the Sanskrit language which support its ability to do this. A summary list of its credentials is in Appendix 1.

Note

1. *The Supreme Yoga: The Yoga Vāsiṣṭha* translated by Swāmi Venkatesānanda, the Chiltern Yoga Trust 1976

Appendix 1

Checklist of the credentials of the Sanskrit language considered in this book.

1. The elemental sounds of the language as expressed in the alphabet have special power, purity and order.
2. These sounds are always directly reflected in written forms.
3. The sound *a*, the first letter of the alphabet, from which all other vowels are shown to arise, pervades the whole language.
4. *Sandhi* operates within and between words, maintaining harmony, stability and integrity of the language.
5. Words are formed in completely lawful ways from *dhātu*s and *pratyaya*s.
6. Words are traced back to *dhātu*s.
7. Words in Sanskrit have fluidity of form, reflecting both the *dhātu*s from which they originate, and the natural fluidity of their effects in the world of meanings.
8. The natural unity of a sentence held in its *sphoṭa*, is expressed through (a) the principle of *kāraka* which governs relationships within the sentence, and is present in most suffixes, not just case endings, and (b) the uniting of sounds through *sandhi*.
9. The vocabulary of the language relates fully to all three worlds, and new words maintain the integrity of the language by being formed in accordance with its grammatical laws.
10. The coherence and stability of Sanskrit grammatical and phonetic laws are indications of a language formed and used with a higher level of consciousness than languages which keep changing in accordance with local customs and practices.

Appendix 2

The extent of Sandhi

THE principles of *Sandhi* are referred to a number of times in this book, but nowhere did it seem appropriate to break off from the general topic being considered and talk about them and their practical operation. This appendix provides that opportunity, not only in language but also in other areas.

This process of *sandhi* can be seen as one of the fundamental principles of the universe because of its widespread nature. Essentially it is concerned with harmonising and creating. The *Taittirīya* Upanishad identifies four elements in the process, and gives some examples. These four elements are: *pūrva*, the one before; *uttara*, the one following; *sandhi*, that which joins; and *sandhānam*, the act of uniting. The whole process is called *saṁhitā,* but the word commonly used is *sandhi*, no doubt because that appears to be the most significant element.

Two of the examples given in the Upanishad are:

1. Teaching: the teacher *(pūrva)*; the student *(uttara)*; knowledge *(sandhi)*; instruction (*sandhānam*).
2. Generation: mother (*pūrva)*, father (*uttara*), progeny (*sandhi*), act of birth (*sandhānam*).

Sandhi in Sanskrit

We have already seen *sandhi* operating in language, more particularly in the Sanskrit language. The four elements as applied in language are the sound before (the *pūrva*), the sound following (the *uttara*), the space between them (the *sandhi*) and the sound which joins them (the *sandhānam*). Here are a couple of examples showing how the four elements come together:

1. When one of the vowels *i, u, ṛ* or *ḷ* is followed by any vowel other than the same vowel, it is replaced by the relevant semi-vowel (*anthaḥstha*) *y, r, l* or *v*. By 'relevant' is meant that sound which is nearest in mouth position to the vowel being replaced. Thus *i* plus *a* becomes *ya*, *y* being the only semi-vowel with the same mouth position as the vowel *i*. The four elements in this case are: *i*, the one before, the *pūrva*; *a*, the one following, the *uttara*; the space between them, which joins them, the *sandhi*; and *y*, the act of uniting, the *sandhānam*. In *u* plus *o* the result would be *vo*.
2. When *m* is the last letter in a word and the following word begins with a consonant, the *m* is replaced by the nasal consonant which has the same mouth position as the following consonant. Thus *aham dadāmi* (I give) becomes *ahandadāmi*. Here *m* is the one before, *d* is the one following, the space between is what joins them, and *n* unites them.

There are several types of *sandhi* in Sanskrit, called vowel, consonant and *visarga sandhi*. These can be distinguished further. In vowel *sandhi* the first vowel, the following vowel or even both vowels, may be replaced by another sound, the *sandhānam*. The same three situations can apply in consonant *sandhi,* with the first, the following or both consonants being replaced. There are also two other situations. A new consonant may appear between the first and the following letters. For example *sam* and *kṛta* become *saṁskṛta* with the augment *s* appearing. *Sandhi* also applies when a consonant is followed by a pause, as at the end of a sentence. In those cases a final voiced consonant will be replaced by an unvoiced one e.g *d* by *t* and *g* by *k*.

In *visarga sandhi* the function of *sandhi* is not simply to produce a harmonious sound, but also to assist with clarity of meaning. Without this process it would often not be possible to distinguish the case of a particular word. In *visarga sandhi* a new sound, a particular *r* called *ru* (the *u* being an *it* letter), comes in to replace the *pūrva* which is usually a final *s* . But in all situations apart from one, this *ru* is then replaced by another sound. *Ru* is an essential part of the process of *visarga sandhi* and acts like a catalyst, as it comes, causes a change, and then departs, not being present in the final form.

Sandhi in the community

There are many examples of *sandhi* in human society.

1. Treaties between nations: (a) *Pūrva.* One nation; (b) *Uttara.* The other nation; (c)*Sandhi.* Speech; (d) *Sandhānam.* Negotiation producing agreement.
2. Marriage: (a) one person; (b) the other person; (c) love; (d) act of marriage.
3. Football match: (a) one team; (b) the other team; (c) rules of the game, as embodied in the referee; (d) the act of playing the match.
4. Court case: (a) the prosecuting party; (b) the defendant; (c) the law –as embodied in judge and jury and court system; (d) the decision –the act of the court.
5. Preparation of a meal: (a) food; (b) cooking implements including oven; (c) the cook; (d) the act of cooking.
6. A house sale: (a) the seller; (b) the prospective purchaser; (c) the house; (d) the act of purchase or agreement to purchase.

7. Statutory legislation: (a) the Government with its Bill; (b) the Opposition with its amendments and objections; (c) the legislative process of debates through both Houses of Parliament; (d) agreement of the Act of Parliament.
8. Rehearsal of a play: (a) the actors (b) the management team including the director, the theatre owner etc: (c) the play; (d) the rehearsal.
9. Performance of a play: (a) actors and management; (b) the audience; (c) the play; (d) the performance.
10. The economy: (a) land; (b) man's ability to work; (c) conditions at the point of interaction; (d) act of production.

When one of these elements is either not present or not operating properly, then *sandhi* does not take place. For instance the first example above could end in war, the second in breaking off the engagement, the fourth in no decision, the sixth in absence of a sale, and the seventh in an Act of Parliament which is unworkable, maybe because the Government paid no attention to arguments in the House and simply used its majority to force through the Bill.

Sandhi in science

Chemical reactions can be seen as processes of *sandhi.* Atoms are stable, but metals and non-metals have a tendency to be positively or negatively charged due to their inherent atomic structures. This causes them to become unstable in the presence of some other atoms. This can lead to bonding, giving an overall neutrality in the new structure. The positive and negative forces are contained within the new structure and help to maintain the stability of that structure. For example when the elements zinc and sulphur are heated together, there is a chemical reaction which produces zinc sulphate, a substance which has qualities quite different from either zinc or sulphur. Here zinc and sulphur, the *pūrva* and *uttara*, are bonded in heat, the *sandhi,* and the chemical reaction is the *sandhānam.* Similarly hydrogen bonded with oxygen through heating produces water. In other chemical reactions the substances will be different and the *sandhi* could be different, but the principle would be the same.

Living processes appear to use the principle of *sandhi,* such as respiration, photosynthesis, carbohydrate formation, protein formation and nitrogen fixation (essentially nitrogen and hydrogen heated to form ammonia).

The common feature in all these areas of *sandhi* operation is the force for balance, for harmony. Balance is achieved when two entities come to unity and achieve a certain stability in the material world or harmony in the subtle world. *Sandhi* also has a creative aspect, as new entities can be created by this force for harmony. Maybe this force is relevant to this statement from Śāntānanda Sarasvatī about the realisation of the Self: 'It [realisation] can be instantaneous like a flash, which can transform the being inside and outside... Once realisation has taken place then all actions will naturally become harmonious with the universe.' (Day 1 1989)

Bibliography
(principal references)

Abhyankar K. V. and Shukla J. M., *A Dictionary of Sanskrit Grammar,* Oriental Institute, Baroda, 1977

Aṣṭādhyāyī of Pāṇini, ed and trans Vasu S.C., Motilal Banarsidass, 1891

Baugh A.C., *A History of the English Language,* Routledge & Kegan Paul, 1959

Bhagavad Gītā, with commentary of Shankara, trans Swami Gambhirananda, Advaita Ashrama,1991, and other translations

Bragg M., *The Adventure of English,* Hodder & Stoughton, 2003

Burrow T., *The Sanskrit Language,* Faber & Faber, 1955

Cardona G., *Pāṇini. A Survey of Research,* Mouton & Co, 1976

Chomsky N., *Language and Mind,* Cambridge University Press, 2006

Crystal D., *The Cambridge Encyclopedia of Language,* Cambridge University Press, 2003

Chāndogya Upanishad,with commentary of Shankara, trans Gambhirananda S., Advaita Ashrama, 1983

Eight Upanishads,with commentary of Shankara, trans Gambhirananda S., Advaita Ashrama, 1978, and other translations

Iyer K.A.S., *Bhartṛhari,* Deccan College, 1992

Jaiswal S.L., *London Language Lectures 1997-2008,* School of Economic Science, 2009

Jean G., *The Story of Alphabets and Scripts,* Thames Hudson, 1992

Kenny A. (editor), *The Wittgenstein Reader,* Blackwell, 1994

Laghusiddhāntakaumudī of Varadarāja trans Ballantyne J.M., Motilal Banarsidass, 4th edition 1891

Locke J., *An Essay concerning Human Understanding,* Penguin Books, 1997

Murti M.S., *Bhartṛhari the Grammarian,* Sahitya Academy, 1997

Ostler N, *Empires of the Word,* HarperCollins, 2005

Mahābhāṣya Kārakāhnika of Patañjali, ed and notes Joshi S.D. and Roodbergen J., Poona University Press, 1975

Śāntānanda Sarasvatī, Conversations with Leon MacLaren 1965-1993, unpublished, rights reserved

Swami Śankarānanda, *The Yoga of Kashmir Shaivism,* Motilal Banarsidass, 2006

Sharma R.N., *The Aṣṭādhyāyī of Pāṇini,* Munshiram Manoharlal, 1987

Siddhāntakaumudī of Bhaṭṭoji Dīkṣita ed & trans Vasu S.C., Motilal Banarsidass, 1906

Tripathi K.R., *Arrangement of the Rules in Pāṇini's Aṣṭādhyāyī,* Parimal, 1991

The Vākyapadīya of Bhartṛhari, trans and notes Iyer K.A.S., Motilal Banarsidass. 1977

The Way of Hermes trans Salaman C., van Oyen D., Wharton W., Duckworth, 1999

Index

References are to secion of chaper

Advaita 1.7, 2.3, 2.6, 2.10, 3.3, 3.8, 4.1, 4.6, 4.8, 5.3, 5.4, 5.6, 6.3, 7.1, 7.4, 7.7, 7.8, 8.1, 8.6
- summary of 1.1
- and language 1.2, 4.1
affix – see *pratyaya*
alphabet 1.2, 2.3-10, 3.1-12, 4.2, 5.3, 6.4, 7.2, 8.4, App 1
analytical languages 2.2, 2.3, 2.9, 2.10, 5.2
a sound 2.4, 2.5, 3.2, 3.3, 3.5, 4.4, 8.2, App 1
Ātman – see Self
Aurobindo 3.2

Bhartṛhari 1.2, 1.5, 4.1, 4.8, 5.2, 5.3, 6.2, 6.8, 8.5
Bhagavad Gītā 3.4, 5.4
Brahman 1.1, 1.2, 2.10, 3.3, 4.6, 6.7

case ending – see *vibhakti*
causal world 1.1, 2.8, 3.3, 3.13, 6.2, 6.5, 7.4, 7.6, 8.5
chakra 3.5, 3.13, 5.3
Chomsky, Noam 1.5, 7.1
compound word 2.8, 3.10, 4.7, 4.11
consciousness 1.1, 1.2, 1.5, 2.3, 2.7, 2.10, 3.4, 3.5, 3.8, 4.1, 5.2, 5.3, 5.6, 6.4, 7.5, 8.5, App 1
consonant 2.2, 3.2-7, 3.12, App 2

Dante 6.2
dharma – see natural law
dhātu 2.3-5, 2.8, 3.7-9, 3.13, 4.2-10, 5.3, 5.6, 6.4, 6.6, 7.2, 7.3, 7.5, 8.2, 8.5, App 1
Dhātupaṭha 4.3-5, 6.1
empiricism 1.4, 1.6, 6.3
English language 2.2-10, 3.7-13, 4.2, 4.3, 4.5, 5.5, 6.3

grammar 1.2-4, 2(all), 3.1, 3.6, 3.10, 4.3, 5.4
- generative 1.5, 7.1
- and meaning 6.6, 6.8
- morphology and syntax 3.1
- Sanskrit 2.9, 4.1-4, 5.4, 6.6, 7 (all), 8.2, App 1
- universal (deep) 1.5, 5.4, 7.1

inflectional languages 2.2, 2.3, 2.9, 2.10, 4.2, 5.2
It letters 4.4, 7.2, 7.7, 7.8

kāraka 3.10, 3.13, 4.4, 4.8, 4.9, 5.4, 6.6, 7.4, 7.5, 7.8, App 1

law and lawfulness 2.3, 2.6, 2.10, 5.4, 8.3
- see also natural law
Locke, John 1.4, 6.2
logical positivism 1.4

MacLaren, Leon 4.7, 5.3
madhyamā stage of speech 4.11, 5.3
*Māheśvara sutra*s 3.6, 3.12, 3.13, 7.2
Mandarin Chinese 2.2-10
material world 1.1, 2.8, 3.3, 3.11, 3.13, 4.1, 6.2, 7.4, 7.6, 8.5
mātrikā 3.3
mental world – see subtle world

natural language 1.2, 6.3, 6.4, 7.8
natural law 1.2, 4.3, 7.3, 8.1, 8.3
noun 2.3, 3.8, 3.10, 4.2, 4.4 –9, 5.4, 5.6, 6.6, 7.5
noun case affix 2.4, 3.10, 4.2, 4.4, 4.7, 4.9, 5.4

Om ॐ 1.2, 3.3, 4.1, 4.7, 5.3, 6.3, 6.4

Pāṇini 3.4, 3.6, 3.11, 4.4, 4.5, 5.4, 7 (all)
parā stage of speech 4.11, 5.3, 5.6
Patañjali 3.4, 3.8, 4.8, 5.3, 6.4
paśyantī stage of speech 4.11, 5.3
phonetics 1.3, 3.1, 3.6, 8.4
physical world
– see material world
Plato 1.3, 1.5, 1.6, 6.6
prakṛti 3.4, 3.8
pratibhā 5.2, 6.8
prātipadika 3.10, 4.2, 4.4, 7.3
pratyāhāra 3.6, 3.12
pratyaya 2.3-5, 2.8, 3.8, 3.10, 3.13, 4.3, 4.4, 4.9, 5.3, 5.4, 5.6, 6.4, 6.6, 7.3, 7.5, 8.5, App 1
prefix 2.4, 3.9, 3.13, 4.3, 4.5, 4.9
puruṣa 2.8, 3.4, 3.8, 4.6

rationalism 1.4 – 6
reflection, reflectivity 1.1, 1.2, 2.3, 2.8, 2.10, 4.1, 4.11, 6.3, 6.4, 7.7, 7.8, 8.5
root – see *dhātu*
samāsa – see compound word
Sānkhya philosophy 3.8
sandhi 2.3, 2.4, 3.12, 3.13, 4.4, 5.5, 8.2, 8.3, 8.5, App 1, App 2
– examples 7.3, App 2
Sanskrit language 2(all), 3(all), 4(all), 5.2, 5.4, 5.5, 6.1, 6.4, 6.5, 7(all), 8.1-5, App 1& 2
Self (*Ātman)* 1.1, 2.10, 3.8, 4.1, 4.6, 5.4 - 6, 6.7, 7.4, 8.5, App 2
sentence 1.2, 2.2, 2.4, 3.10, 4.2, 4.3, 5 (all), 6.2, 6.6, 6.8, 7.4, 8.2
Shāntānanda Sarasvatī 1.2, 2.7, 3.3, 3.6, 5.3, 5.6, 6.2-5, 6.7, 8.4, App 2
sound 1.2, 2.2 – 5, 2.7, 2.9, 2.10, 3 (all), 4.1, 5.5, 5.6, 6.3-6, 6.8, 8.4, App 1
sphoṭa 1.2, 4.1, 5.2, 5.3, 5.5, 6.8, 8.2
spiritual world – see causal world
stability 2.3, 2.4, 2.9, 2.10, 8.3, App 2
stem of word – see *prātipadika*
subtle world 1.1, 2.8, 3.3, 3.11, 3.13, 4.1, 6.2, 6.8, 7.4, 7.6, 8.5
suffix – see *pratyaya*

unity – see *Advaita*
– in a language 2.3, 2.10, 3.11, 4.5, 4.6, 5.2, 5.3, 5.6, 7.7, 8.2
Upanishad 2.7, 6.5, 7.3
– *Chāndogya* 1.2, 6.2, 6.3
– *Māṇḍūkya* 1.2, 6.3
– *Taittirīya* App 2

vaikharī stage of speech 4.11, 5.3, 5.6
Vedangas 1.3, 3.1
verb 2.3, 3.8, 3.10, 4.2, 4.4 –9, 5.1, 5.4, 5.6, 6.6, 7.5
verbal affixes 2.4, 4.2, 4.4, 4.9, 5.4, 7.5, 7.7
vibhakti – i.e. noun and verbal affixes 2.4, 3.10, 4.4, 4.7, 4.9, 5.4, 7.5, 7.7
vowel 2.2, 2.5, 3.2-7, 3.12, App 2

Wittgenstein, Ludwig 1.6, 5.2, 6.7
word 1.1-6, 2.2-4, 2.6, 2.8, 2.10, 3.7–11, 4 (all), 5 (all), 6.2, 6.6 – 8, 7.3, 8.5
worlds
– see causal, subtle, material